SpringerBriefs in Law

More information about this series at http://www.springer.com/series/10164

Jonathan Herring

Vulnerability, Childhood and the Law

Springer

Jonathan Herring
Faculty of Law, Exeter College
University of Oxford
Oxford
UK

ISSN 2192-855X ISSN 2192-8568 (electronic)
SpringerBriefs in Law
ISBN 978-3-319-78685-8 ISBN 978-3-319-78686-5 (eBook)
https://doi.org/10.1007/978-3-319-78686-5

Library of Congress Control Number: 2018937348

© The Author(s) 2018
This work is subject to copyright. All rights are reserved by the Publisher, whether the whole or part of the material is concerned, specifically the rights of translation, reprinting, reuse of illustrations, recitation, broadcasting, reproduction on microfilms or in any other physical way, and transmission or information storage and retrieval, electronic adaptation, computer software, or by similar or dissimilar methodology now known or hereafter developed.
The use of general descriptive names, registered names, trademarks, service marks, etc. in this publication does not imply, even in the absence of a specific statement, that such names are exempt from the relevant protective laws and regulations and therefore free for general use.
The publisher, the authors and the editors are safe to assume that the advice and information in this book are believed to be true and accurate at the date of publication. Neither the publisher nor the authors or the editors give a warranty, express or implied, with respect to the material contained herein or for any errors or omissions that may have been made. The publisher remains neutral with regard to jurisdictional claims in published maps and institutional affiliations.

Printed on acid-free paper

This Springer imprint is published by the registered company Springer International Publishing AG part of Springer Nature
The registered company address is: Gewerbestrasse 11, 6330 Cham, Switzerland

Contents

1	**Introduction**	1
1.1	The Central Argument of the Book	1
1.2	The Definition of Childhood	2
1.3	Children's Vulnerability	4
1.4	Protection Under the Criminal Law	5
1.5	Particular Rights	6
1.6	Privileged Status	6
1.7	Conclusion	7
	References	7
2	**What is Vulnerability?**	9
2.1	Introduction	9
2.2	Labelling Groups	9
2.3	Internal and External Elements	10
2.4	Subjective/Objective Understanding of Vulnerability	11
2.5	Official Definitions of Vulnerability	12
2.6	Proposed Definition	13
2.7	Conclusion	14
	References	14
3	**Children and Vulnerability**	17
3.1	Introduction	17
3.2	Why Is Childhood Seen as a Time of Vulnerability?	17
3.3	The Consequences of the Construction of Vulnerability	18
	3.3.1 Paternalism	18
	3.3.2 The Quietening of Children	19
	3.3.3 The Confinement of Children	21
3.4	The Thinness of the Vulnerability Narrative	22
	3.4.1 Selective	22
	3.4.2 Homogenisation	22

v

		3.4.3 Endangerment	23
	3.5	Conclusion	24
	References		24

4 Are Children More Vulnerable Than Adults? ... 27
  4.1 Introduction 27
  4.2 Universal Vulnerability 28
  4.3 We Are All Dependent on Others 31
  4.4 We All Have Impaired Capacity 32
      4.4.1 Information 33
      4.4.2 Rationality 34
      4.4.3 Values 35
      4.4.4 The Exaggerated Significance of Capacity 36
  4.5 The Vulnerability of the Human Body 37
  4.6 The Vulnerable Self 38
  4.7 Care 38
  4.8 Are Children Special? 40
  4.9 The Social Construction of Childhood 42
  4.10 Conclusion 43
  References 44

5 Childhood, Adulthood and the Law 47
  5.1 Introduction 47
  5.2 Our Image of the Legal Self 48
  5.3 Rights 49
  5.4 Divisions 54
  5.5 Vulnerability and Care as Private 55
  5.6 Responsibilities to the Vulnerable 56
  5.7 Age of Consent 59
  5.8 Conclusion 61
  References 62

6 Vulnerability Is Good 65
  6.1 The Good of Vulnerability 65
  6.2 Vulnerability and Co-operation 66
  6.3 Vulnerability and Change 67
  6.4 Vulnerability and Relationships 67
  6.5 Vulnerability and Personhood 69
  6.6 Conclusion 69
  References 70

Chapter 1
Introduction

Abstract This chapter sets out some of the key arguments of the book. It does this by explaining the concept of childhood and how the law interacts with children. It also explore how the law uses age in a range of situations to determine what rights children do or do not have under the law. The chapter also introduces the concept of vulnerability which is used to justify the law's interaction with children.

Keywords Vulnerability · Child · Protection · Rights · Status

1.1 The Central Argument of the Book

This book explores the nature of what it is to be a child, an adult and indeed a person. Foundational to legal and social responses to people is the distinction between children and adults. Your legal rights and social position depend hugely on whether you are classified as an adult or a child. In short for adults the guiding principle is autonomy: you are free to live your life as you choose, as long as you have capacity to make the choice and you are not harming others (Foster 2009). For children, the law protects children from harms and decisions are made by others based on what is in a child's welfare. Determining what will promote a child's welfare is a task that is normally handed over to parents, but where necessary courts can make the assessment (Children Act 1989, Section 1).

Underpinning that distinction between childhood and adulthood is the idea of children being vulnerable and therefore in need of protection; while adults are able to look after themselves. Childhood is seen as a time for safety and preparation for adulthood. It is at the same time a precarious time: the child is seen as at risk to wide range of dangers; but also a precious one: the child is learning skills and having experiences which will have a profound impact on their adult life.

This book will challenge that distinction between children and adulthood. It will do so by exploring the concept of vulnerability which for many writers has been at the heart of justification for why children can, and should, be treated differently from adults. The argument that we should draw no distinction between adults and children is not a new one. Ever since the child liberationist movement in the 1960s, there have been plenty of writers arguing that we underestimate the capacities of children and need to recognise that they can be as competent and able as adults. We need, therefore, to treat children in the same way as adults. This book, however, argues the opposite. Children are vulnerable, as is everyone. In children we adults see our own vulnerability and flee from it. We need to recognise the vulnerabilities of adults. Yes, we should treat children and adults alike, but do so by treating adults more like children not children more like adults.

1.2 The Definition of Childhood

There is no settled definition of childhood. Certainly there is no clear answer in law. The United Nations Convention on the Rights of the Child opens:

> For the purposes of the present Convention, a child means every human being below the age of 18 years unless under the law applicable to the child, majority is attained earlier.

This gives us a maximum age for childhood, but appears to leave the minimum age up to individual countries.

In English law no definite answer as to when childhood ends can be given. There are different ages for different activities. For example

5 years old

- You can have a bank account in own name

7 years old

- You can draw money from Post Office or savings account

10 years old

- You can be convicted of a crime

12 years old

- You can see a film certified as 12A without an adult.

13 years old

- You can get a job for a certain number of hours

14 years old

- You are responsible for your wearing a seatbelt
- You are allowed to ride an electrically assisted bike.

15 years old

- You can see a 15 rated film.

16 years old

- You can get married, providing a person with parental responsivity for you consent.
- You can consent to have sex.
- You can leave school
- With the consent of a parent you can join the armed forces
- You can get a licence to drive a moped
- You join a Trade Union
- You can buy premium bonds and play the National Lottery
- You can drink beer, cider or wine with a meal in a restaurant if accompanied by a person over 18

17 years old

- You can get a licence to drive some vehicles.
- You can be sent to prison
- You can donate blood

18 years old

- You can buy alcohol and tobacco
- You can make a will and act as an executor of a will
- You can get married without your parents' consent.
- You can vote and stand as a candidate in an election
- You can buy fireworks
- You can buy land
- You can consent to have a tattoo

21 years old

- You can drive any mechanically propelled vehicle, if the appropriate tests are passed.
- You can adopt a child

As can be seen from this list it is not possible to identify a single age at which a person crosses the line from being a child to an adult. The division of ages is somewhat strange. For example, you can have sex with your MP at age 16, but cannot vote for them until you are 18!!

So the definition of childhood is left uncertain. As Gilmore and Glennon (2016, 427) explain:

> Who is to be regarded as a child, and consequently the boundary between childhood and adulthood is socially constructed by the law of a particular society.

Brighouse and Swift (2016, 4) suggest that people are seen as children if 'because of their age, have yet to develop the capacities that characterize normal adulthood.' Yet this leaves open the question of what the normal capacities of adulthood are. It also does not quite capture the nature of the adult-child relationship created by the concept of childhood. As Smith (1997, 153) writes:

> We are not prepared to withdraw our protection or to abandon the legal distinction between children and adults. To do so would strike at the very heart of the adult-child relationship which enables adults to locate themselves emotionally, as being affectionate, caring, protective and socially, as being responsible for mounding the next generation of citizens.

In this book, I will focus on what is seen as one of the defining features of childhood: vulnerability.

1.3 Children's Vulnerability

The vulnerability rhetoric surrounding children not only explains the law's response to childhood, it is also a theme prevalent in the portrayal of children in media (Scraton 1997; Valentine 2017). We hear much of 'the crisis in childhood' (Kehily 2010; The Children's Society 2008). In 2006 the then Archbishop of Canterbury attracted considerable attention when he declared that childhood was under threat, being damaged by commercial pressures, family break-down and parents who refuse to grow up (BBC News 2006). This picture of childhood under challenge is a common theme in the literature. Jackson and Scott (1999, 86) write that '[c]hildhood is increasingly being constructed as a precious realm under siege from those who would rob children of their childhoods, and as being subverted from within by children who refuse to remain childlike'. There is even an Open University (2017) Course entitled 'Childhood in Crisis?'

As already indicated it is the vulnerability of children which is usually relied upon to justify the differences in legal treatment between adults and children. In *Re X (A Minor) (Wardship: Jurisdiction)* [1975] Fam 47 Latey J, a wise and experienced family law judge, once said:

> children are especially vulnerable. They have not formed the defences inside themselves which older people have, and, therefore, need especial protection. They are also a country's most valuable asset.

This quote captures two key points about childhood in the legal imagination. Both are connected with the idea that children are especially vulnerable. The first is that they, unlike adults, lack the ability to defend themselves from a wide range of risks. Children are unaware of the risks they face and therefore cannot avoid them. Further, they lack the physical, emotional and social resources to respond effectively to harms if they suffer them. Hence, concerns about child abuse in its many forms, makes people wary of giving children the kinds of rights we give adults, because that would lead to increased exploitation of children (Fortin 2009, 5). Archard (2001, 52) argues 'granting fundamental liberties to a child before he possesses the capacities to be the guardian of his own life is cruel'.

The second, is that children are a "valuable asset". The least important, but most often mentioned, reason for why children are important is that "They are the taxpayers of the future"! They require nurturing and supporting so that they fulfil that promise, rather than become dependent on the state for support. As a result, they also need a broad range of legal and social provisions, such as education and health services, designed to prepare children for self-sufficiency and adulthood.

These legal interventions can be broken down into three primary categories: protection of children under the criminal law; special rights to social provisions; and a privileged status in law. We shall look at each of these separately.

1.4 Protection Under the Criminal Law

There is an extensive range of offences under the criminal law which are specifically aimed at protecting children. Some of these are designed to highlight the severity of the wrong that is done to a child. This can be done through sentencing, where an offence against a child will attract a longer sentence than the same offence if done to an adult (e.g. whole life sentences for murder of a child under Criminal Justice Act 2003, as amended). It can also be done through particular offences, such as Sexual Offences Act 2003, whereby, unusually in the criminal law the characteristic of the victim is seen as justifying a different label of the offence. For example, there is the general offence of rape (Section 1) and then a specific offence of rape of a child under 13 (Section 5).

Some of the most significant protections of criminal law offered to children, relate to consent. There are a host of activities which are offences, unless done with the consent of the victim. Tattooing, sexual activities or surgery would all be unlawful, without the consent of the victim. The question then arises whether or not children have the capacity to consent to the harms. Cases can be broken down into two categories:

1. Those where the consent of the child will be a defence, but only if the child is shown to have capacity.
2. Those where the consent of the child is never a defence, even if the child has capacity.

The first category of cases is not particularly notable. The consent of a child who lacks capacity is as worthless in this context as the consent of anyone else who lacks capacity. Children are, therefore, treated in a similar way to adults. The only point of significance may be that there seems to be a presumption of a lack of capacity in relation to children, while there is a presumption of capacity in relation to adult [Mental Capacity Act 2005, s. 1(2)]. Even this may be a relatively little impact because there will be an assessment of the child by an expert in preparation for the trial. Then the presumption will only rarely be used because the professional will be able to undertake a full assessment for some reason, or the assessment is inconclusive. There may be more relevance in relation to *mens rea*. It may be harder for a defendant to persuade a jury they believed the victim had capacity to consent in relation to a child than it would be in relation to an adult.

It is the second category where there is an age limit, that there is a significant difference in treatment. Even though the child has capacity their consent is ineffective. Significantly this is not a difference that depends on capacity: it is entirely a difference based solely on the fact the individual is a child. Perhaps the best known example of this is that a child under the age of 16 cannot give effective consent to sexual intercourse, even if it is shown the child has the understanding and maturity of an adult.

There are two plausible explanations for what the law is doing in such cases. One is that the law is using age as a proxy for capacity. The law it might be argued commonly has to rely on bright lines and rough and ready proxies. A well-known example is a speed limit, which sets a figure above which it is deemed dangerous to drive. The second, is that the law is openly protecting the child from harm based on their childhood status. In other words there are wrongs done a child, even if they consent, because it harms goods in the nature of childhood, we wish to protect. For example, you might think that innocence is a good of childhood and even if a child wanted to lose their innocence, an adult should not be able to take that innocence away. We will be exploring these issues later in Chap. 3 of this book.

1.5 Particular Rights

It also seems that children have particular rights against the state or privileges in services, which others do not have. The most obvious would be the right to education (European Convention on Human *Rights, Article 2, First Protocol*) which is generally seen as applying for children, but not adults. Another example might be medical services, such as free prescriptions available under the NHS which are not available generally to adults. These can been as justified in part because of the state needs children to develop into worthy citizens, but also because we cannot expect children to provide for these themselves.

1.6 Privileged Status

Children's vulnerability is also seen in the privileging of children's interests when disputes arise concerning the upbringing of children. We can see this in English law, with the well know paramountcy principle in Section 1 of the Children Act 1989 (Herring 2005): This states:

(1) When a court determines any question with respect to—

    (a) the upbringing of a child; or
    (b) the administration of a child's property or the application of any income arising from it,

the child's welfare shall be the court's paramount consideration.

The reference to paramount consideration has been subject to quite some academic debate (Herring 1999), but it is generally taken to mean that the courts should focus on the welfare of the child, and not consider the interests of adults (Eekelaar 2002).

This especial privileging of children is found in many jurisdictions. The United Nations Convention on the Rights of the Child, Article 3 states:

> In all actions concerning children, whether undertaken by public or private social welfare institutions, courts of law, administrative authorities or legislative bodies, the best interests of the child shall be a primary consideration.

This is generally taken to be slightly difference from the paramountcy principle in the Children Act 1989 as it accepts that the interests of adults can be a consideration. Nevertheless it makes it clear that children's interests rank higher than those of adults. We will be exploring the possible reasons for this privileging of children's interests in Chap. 3.

1.7 Conclusion

This chapter has sought to outline the crucial distinction drawn in the law between adults and children. Children are given a range of rights not given to adults; they are subject to restrictions on their freedom, in order to protect them from harm; and their interests are given special privilege in legal disputes, as compared with adults. The justification for this treatment is vulnerability. As Norozi and Moen (2016) put it:

> children are viewed as those who are physically weaker, less well-developed, weigh less than adults. Children are considered those who need to get the developmental stages of secondary sexual features in order to be called an adult. Children tend to have less cognitive skills, intellectual abilities, less knowledge, less ability for reasoning. Children are deliberated as those who have less emotional maturity and less socially skilled. Children are contemplated as those with less competence in terms of life-skills and less expressive. Children are perceived as relatively in powerless position in relation to adults.

In the chapters ahead I will argue against the view promoted in this quote. Adults are as lacking in capacity, intellectual ability, emotional maturity and power as children are.

References

Archard D (2001) Philosophical perspectives on childhood. In: Fiona J (ed) Legal concepts of childhood. Oxford University Press, Oxford
BBC News (2006) Childhood 'in crisis'. 18 Sept 2006
Brighouse H, Swift A (2016) Family values. Princeton University Press, Princeton, NJ

Eekelaar J (2002) Beyond the welfare principle. Child and Family Law Quarterly 14:237–252
Fortin J (2009) Children's rights and the developing law. Cambridge University Press, Cambridge
Foster C (2009) Choosing life, choosing death. Hart, Oxford
Gilmore S, Glennon L (2016) Family law. Oxford University Press, Oxford
Herring J (1999) The human rights act and the welfare principle in family law—conflicting or complementary? Child and Family Law Quarterly 11:223–243
Herring J (2005) Farewell welfare. Journal of Social Welfare and Family Law 27:159–173
Jackson S, Scott S (1999) Risk anxiety and the social construction of childhood. In: Lupton D (ed) Risk and sociocultural theory: new directions and perspectives. Cambridge University Press, Cambridge
Kehily M (2010) Childhood in crisis? tracing the contours of 'crisis' and its impact upon contemporary parenting practices. Media Culture Society 32:171–186
Norozi S, Moen T (2016) Childhood as a social construction. Journal of Educational and Social Research 6:75–102
Open University (2017) http://www.open.edu/openlearn/health-sports-psychology/childhood-youth/childhood-crisis/content-section-0. Last accessed 19 Jan 2018
Scraton P (ed) (1997) Childhood in crisis. Sage, London
Smith C (1997) Children's rights: judicial ambivalence and social relations. International Journal of Law, Policy and the Family 11:103
The Children's Society (2008) Children: good childhood inquiry report debate. Children's Society, London
Valentine G (2017) Public space and the culture of childhood. Routledge, ch 1

Chapter 2
What is Vulnerability?

Abstract This chapter explores the concept of vulnerability. The special legal position of children is commonly justified by vague references to them being particularly vulnerable. This chapter will examine the different facets of vulnerability. In particular, it will highlight the objective and subjective aspects of vulnerability; and the extent to which the source of vulnerability can be seen as external or internal to the individual.

Keywords Vulnerability · Status · Objectivity · Internal · External

2.1 Introduction

In Chap. 1 I highlighted how the notion of vulnerability is at the heart of the distinction the law draws between adults and children. It is children's vulnerability which justifies the protections given them by the law; the restrictions on their freedom; the especial rights they have as against the state; and the privileging of their rights in relation to legal proceedings. In this chapter, I will explore in more detail the nature and meaning of vulnerability.

The notion of vulnerability is used in many disciplines and without a consistent meaning (Dunn et al. 2008). According to the Oxford Dictionary of English (2010), to be vulnerable means 'to be exposed to the possibility of being attacked or harmed, either physically or emotionally.' That seems an extremely broad understanding. You would need to stay in bed very firmly wrapped up in your duvet to escape the possibility of being harmed! However, it does capture a core idea about vulnerability: that it is about being exposed to risks.

2.2 Labelling Groups

Currently, it is common currently for vulnerability to be used in relation to particular groups or individuals. For example, if a medical researcher has a volunteer from a member of a vulnerable group, this will automatically trigger a set of mechanisms to ensure that the volunteer is protected and freely consenting, or may indeed prohibit a member of that group (Kipnis 2001).

There are benefits to labelling certain groups as vulnerable and need of especial attention. When an individual or organisation has to deal with a large group of people, an individual assessment of the needs and understanding of every individual may be too time consuming; too costly; and even invasive or privacy. Alerting organisations or individual to particular categories of people who are seen as vulnerable and needing an especial protections or assessments. It can also ensure protection for a group when a generalised assessment of vulnerability may not be effective. For example, a woman who has just given birth will be visited by a health worker and assessed for signs of post-natal depression. That is because depression is particularly linked with post-birth life. If new mothers were not identified as such a vulnerable group, it may well be that many cases would not be identified.

However, the "vulnerable group" approach carries dangers. These have been summarized in this way:

> [T]he concept of vulnerability stereotypes whole categories of individuals, without distinguishing between individuals in the group who indeed might have special characteristics that need to be taken into account and those who do not. Particular concerns have been raised about considering all poor people, all pregnant women, all members of ethnic or racial minorities, and all people with terminal illness as inherently vulnerable (Levine et al. 2004, 45).

A couple of things are notable about such a view point. First, it assumes that being labelled as vulnerable is something negative. As already mentioned, it reflects a false elevation of autonomy and independence as desirable states. Second, it is perhaps an unfair characterization of how such labelling can be used. It may not be being used as a way of saying that every member of that group is especially vulnerable. It may just be alerting an organization or decision-maker to the fact that people in that group may need particular services or help.

2.3 Internal and External Elements

There are two aspects of vulnerability which it is worth developing at this point. First, there are external elements: forces from outside that threaten harm to the individual. They may come from other people or be natural forces, such as weather. Second, there are internal elements: the ability to protect oneself from these forces. This element means that someone may be vulnerable to an external element, but be able to protect themselves from it or respond to it. There may, therefore, be a range of resources a person can draw on to be resilient to a threat or to be able to avoid it (Hurst 2004).

Schroeder and Gefenas (2009) capture these two elements of vulnerability in this way:

> To be vulnerable means to face a significant probability of incurring an identifiable harm while substantially lacking ability and/or means to protect oneself.

2.3 Internal and External Elements

The distinction between external risks and internal capabilities to respond to the risk is helpful, but it is not a watertight distinction. An individual characteristic can only be a source of vulnerability in the context of particular social circumstances. Being unable to walk might, or might not, render one at greater risk of being mugged depending on a wide range of social circumstances (Hurst 2004). There being high level of pollen in the air might not create a risk of harm to most people, but it will for those whose bodies are particularly sensitive to pollen.

2.4 Subjective/Objective Understanding of Vulnerability

A further distinction which can be helpful in understanding vulnerability concerns the perspective from which the risk is assessed. Dunn et al. (2008) distinguish 'etic' and 'emic' understandings of vulnerability:

> 'Etic' approaches equate vulnerability with risk, and assess an individual's vulnerability in terms of the risk facing that person, justifying intervention as a means of managing that risk with regard to objectively determined standards [Aday 2001].
>
> 'Emic' approaches, in contrast, are based on the experiential perception of 'exposure to harm through challenges to one's integrity… [It] places vulnerability in a psycho-socialcultural context' [Spiers 2000], and focus on the subjective reality of a person's everyday life…. [V]ulnerability exists as lived experience. The individual's perception of self and challenges to self, and of resources to withstand such challenges, define vulnerability'.

This distinction is helpful because it opens up the possibility of recognising that what might be regarded as vulnerability from the outside perspective might not be so regarded by the individual. Similarly, a person might perceive themselves to be vulnerable to a risk, which they are not, objectively, facing. This means it is necessary to listen to the voice of the person that is said to be disadvantaged to ascertain what it means to be vulnerable. A good example might be the hearing of voices by someone from someone with Schizophrenia. To an external observer this might be a source of risk, but the individual the voice might be seen as a source of comfort and even a resource to cope with life (Living with Schizophrenia 2017). Similarly a hoarder might find comfort in their cluttered existence, while an external observer may find risks of infection and restrictions of lifestyle (Royal College of Psychiatrists 2017).

The benefit of this analysis is that it can, as Dunn et al. (2008) emphasise, ensure that the individual is at the heart of the intervention. Williams (2008) uses the example of an elderly couple who live with their son. Every now and then the son takes money from their wallet without asking them and uses it to buy a drink. That might look like a clear case of financial abuse. However, imagine the couple are aware of this. They are aware that their care imposes a burden on their son, but he would never ask for money for fear that would make them feel awkward. They leave their wallet out in an open place so the money can be taken. To them the removal of the money is a convenient way of providing him treats, which would be awkward if done more openly. Objectively it might appear to be a case where the couple are vulnerable (to financial abuse), but once their perspective is taken into account, there must be a reassessment of whether they are vulnerable. That is not to mean that there is no weight attached to the objective assessment, but that both perspectives should be considered.

2.5 Official Definitions of Vulnerability

To find a definition of vulnerability, we might draw on definitions in official documents. The well-known, but now abandoned, definition of a vulnerable adult in the *No Secrets* report (Department of Health 2000, 8) is as follows:

> [A vulnerable adult is a person] who is or may be in need of community care services by reason of mental or other disability, age or illness; and who is or may be unable to take care of him or herself, or unable to protect him or herself against significant harm or exploitation.

This definition notably ties the understanding of being vulnerable with being a person who is need of services by the state. A similar approach can be found in the Safeguarding Vulnerable Groups Act 2006, which views a person to be a vulnerable adult if they have attained the age of eighteen and he or she:

(a) is in residential accommodation
(b) is in sheltered housing
(c) receives domiciliary care
(d) receives any form of health care
(e) is detained in lawful custody
(f) is by virtue of an order of a court under supervision by a person exercising functions for the purposes of Part 1 of the Criminal Justice and Court Services Act 2000 (c. 43)
(g) receives a welfare service of a prescribed description
(h) receives any service or participates in any activity provided specifically for persons who fall within subsection (9)
(i) payments are made to him (or to another on his behalf) in pursuance of arrangements under section 57 of the Health and Social Care Act 2001 (c. 15), or
(j) requires assistance in the conduct of his affairs (s. 59(1)).

This is a very broad definition. Sub-section (d)'s reference to 'receives any form of health care', is defined as receiving 'treatment, therapy or palliative care of any description' (s. 59(5)). Taking an aspirin seems to fall within that definition. Certainly it seems to assume that a disabled person is automatically vulnerable. This might be edging towards the argument in this book that being vulnerable is an inevitable part of being human. However, it would seem very wide if it was seeking to define a particularly vulnerable group.

Kipnis (2001) in a much quoted analysis suggests there are seven types of vulnerability. Before listing these it is important to note that these were in the context of medical research and so primarily focused on impediments to giving consent:

(1) cognitive: the ability to understand information and make decisions;
(2) jurisdictional: being under the legal authority of someone such as a prison warden;
(3) deferential: customary obedience to medical or other authority;
(4) medical: having an illness for which there is no treatment;
(5) allocational: poverty, educational deprivation;
(6) infrastructure: limits of the research setting to carry out the protocol; and
(7) social: belonging to a socially undervalued group.

This list is helpful because it gives good examples of the difficulties in identifying vulnerability. Take, for example, the category of an illness. Historically we can see what were regarded as illnesses (e.g. homosexuality) would now be regarded as simply a construction by those particular societies. Similarly what constitutes an ability to understand information is a product of a particular mind and assessment of that by social forces. What might today constitute a learning disability, due to its impact on reading or maths, might not even have been recognized as such several hundred years ago when there was less formal education and information was less commonly communicated in writing. Similarly, the list indicates how the existence of social provisions can create or mitigate vulnerabilities.

2.6 Proposed Definition

I suggest that the literature on vulnerability typically takes three unifying elements which capture a core notion of vulnerability. P is vulnerable if the following three factors are present (Herring 2016; Alwang et al. 2001)

1. P faces a risk of harm.
2. P does not have the resource to be able to avoid the risk of harm materializing.
3. P would not be able to adequately respond to the harm if the risk materialized.

The first requirement is that P faces a risk of harm. Clearly if the risk is of something that is not harmful there is no vulnerability. The risk of winning of the lottery does not make one vulnerable! Similarly, in Britain we would not say a person is vulnerable because they are at risk of harm from a tornado, because tornadoes are so rare that it is not a meaningful risk.

The second requirement considers whether a person is easily able to avoid the risk materializing. It may be that there is a serious risk of harm, but P can easily be expected to avoid it by taking steps to avoid it. For example, P is at risk of an infection, but can avoid that risk by being inoculated against it; or there is readily available medication which cures the illness rapidly.

The third point recognizes that some people will be easily able to mitigate the harm; while others will not. For example, a damage to a piece of property may be of little problem to P if she has insurance and can quickly obtain a replacement; but may be a significant problem to a person with no insurance and limited economic resources. It is here that the state provision may be particularly significant. Our society provides extensive protection against some harms, but not others. The opportunity to mitigate the loss through insurance is only available to the wealthy.

As this demonstrates, although all people may face similar risks, it may be that opportunities to avoid the risk materializing or responding to it if it does materialize, may differ from person to person; and particularly from society and society.

2.7 Conclusion

This chapter has explored the concept of vulnerability. It has argued that vulnerability refers to the combination of three features: that a person is at risk of suffering harm; they lacks the resilience and resources to avoid the harm occurring; and lack the resources to respond to the harm if it did materialise.

References

Aday L (2001) At risk in America: The health and health care needs of vulnerable populations in the United States. Jossey-Bass, San Francisco

Alwang J, Siegel Steen P, Jørgensen S (2001) Vulnerability: a view from different disciplines (world bank social protection discussion paper 115). World Bank, Washington

Brown K, Ecclestone K, Emme N (2017) The many faces of vulnerability. Soc Policy Soc 16:497–510

Department of Health (2000) No Secrets. Department of Health, London

Dunn M, Clare I, Holland A (2008) To empower or to protect? Constructing the 'vulnerable adult' in English law and public policy. Legal Studies 28:234–254

Herring J (2016) Vulnerable adults and the law. Oxford University Press, Oxford

Hurst S (2004) Vulnerability in research and health care. Describing the elephant in the room? Med Health Care Philos 7:281–295

Kipnis K (2001) Vulnerability in research subjects: a bioethical taxonomy. In: Ethical and policy issues in research involving human research participants. National Bioethics Advisory Commission, Washington

Levine C, Faden R, Grady C, Hammerschmidt D, Eckenwiler L, Sugarman J (2004) The limitations of "vulnerability" as a protection for human research participants. Am J Bioeth 4:44–50

Living with Schizophrenia (2017) Understanding voices. Living with Schizophrenia, London

References

Oxford English Dictionary (2010) Oxford University Press, Oxford

Royal College of Psychiatrists (2017) Hoarding. Royal College of Psychiatrists, London

Schroeder D, Gefenas E (2009) Vulnerability too vague and too broad. Camb Q Healthc Ethics 18:113

Spiers J (2000) New perspectives on vulnerability using emic and etic approaches. J Adv Nurs 31:715–724

Williams J (2008) State responsibility and the abuse of vulnerable older people: is there a case for a public law to protect vulnerable older people from abuse? In: Bridgeman J, Keating H, Lind C (eds) Responsibility, law and family. Ashgate, Aldershot

Chapter 3
Children and Vulnerability

Abstract This chapter considers the ways in which children are perceived to be vulnerable. It is argued that this perception creates real harm for children. It encourages overly-paternalistic interventions in the lives of children; it means that children are not listened to properly; and that children's liberty is infringed. It claims that, ironically, the treatment of children as particularly vulnerable in fact creates dangers for children.

Keywords Vulnerability · Childhood · Paternalism · Endangerment
Confinement

3.1 Introduction

In this chapter I will explore how vulnerability has been connected to childhood. I will argue that it has been key to how we understand childhood. Indeed, in a sense it can be seen as almost definitional. To be a child is to be vulnerable and in need of protection. To be an adult is to be invulnerable and self-sufficient. An adult who is seen to be vulnerable is often described as "childlike" and subject to the best interests test which dominates the law (Meyer 2007). A child who can demonstrate that they are able to make decisions for themselves can begin escapes the legal regime that attaches to children and start to be treated like an adult.

3.2 Why Is Childhood Seen as a Time of Vulnerability?

Meyer (2007) usefully separates out the alleged forms of childhood vulnerability into three categories: physical, social and structural. These are readily understandable. Physical vulnerability refers to the suggestion that children's bodies tend to be weaker and smaller than adults. Many adults can pick up a child; not many children can pick up and adult. The social vulnerability refers to the fact that children are said to lack the social skills, experiences and relational contexts to protect themselves from harm. The reference to structural vulnerabilities refers to

© The Author(s) 2018
J. Herring, *Vulnerability, Childhood and the Law*, SpringerBriefs in Law,
https://doi.org/10.1007/978-3-319-78686-5_3

the argument that children have limited access to resources such as transport, food and medical care, especially without adults to enable their access. Further, children are taught to be wary of adulthood and the multiple dangers they face, which it is said they are unable to protect themselves from.

It would be wrong to say that children are only described in terms that relate to vulnerability. Children can also be seen as evil; innocent; dangerous; and sources of potential (Piper 2008). Indeed, many commentators have noted the contradictory descriptions of children. For example, their innocence is emphasised when children are seen as the victims of crime and their evil nature when viewed as perpetrators (Valentine 1996). We have seen in recent times these combine so that children who commit crime or anti-social behaviour are subject to increasingly stringent control, whereas at the same time anti-social behaviour challenges children's innocence and is deemed to require ever increasing regulation and protection. These conflicting discourses, however, in fact contribute to their vulnerability.

Children's position is ambiguous in society leaving them open to being ignored when they need protection, or controlled, when they need liberating. I would support Anneke Meyer's (2007, 93) argument that the notion of innocence and vulnerability combine to provide childhood a form of 'moral rhetoric' meaning that 'children and childhood function to explain and legitimize any practice or opinion as right while removing the necessity to provide reasons: children are the reason.'

I will now explore the impact of this vulnerability image of children.

3.3 The Consequences of the Construction of Vulnerability

The current construction of vulnerability has three particular consequences for the law's interaction with childhood that I wish to emphasise.

3.3.1 Paternalism

Part of seeing children as vulnerable means they are seen as open to a range of harms that adults do not face and they lack the resources to respond to those harms. Adults are presented as being in a position to protect children from the harm and to help them cope with any harms they do befall. This role of adults as protector is used, ironically, to mean that adults are permitted to use force to ensure children are protected (Children Act 1989, Section 58). Nikolas Rose (1989, 121) explains:

> The modern child has become the focus of innumerable projects that purport to safeguard it from physical, sexual and moral danger, to ensure its 'normal' development, to actively promote certain capacities of attributes such as intelligence, education and emotional stability.

This is most apparent in the law's granting of parental authority to control, discipline and organise their children. Remarkably parents are permitted to use force, short of actual bodily harm, to discipline a child, when the use of such force

3.3 The Consequences of the Construction of Vulnerability

against an adult will certainly amount to a criminal offence (Children Act 1989, Section 58). Indeed it is seen as one of the key roles of those with parental responsibility to nurture and protect children (Taffel and Blau 1999). So much so that those parents who fail to protect or nurture their children can face criminal sanctions (Children and Young Persons Act 1933). There is a degree of irony here as, in fact, children are far more often abuse by their families, than by strangers.

The ultimate goal of the parental intervention is that in due course the child can move beyond childhood become a rational and full adult citizen (Kaganas and Diduck 2004). They are in this role supported by the requirement that children received education (Education Act 1996, Section 7). But, it is not just parents or schools who have this function. As James et al. (2008) put it:

> [T]he Law operates as one of the main regulatory devices that shape the space of childhood. It does this through developing social policies… that seek to control the kinds of activities that children can do; the social and material environments they inhabit and the resources they have access to.

There is a wide range of mechanisms that are designed to encourage children to become obedient. Indeed, a child being out of the control of her parents is the only ground apart from the risk of significant harm that justifies the court making a care or supervision order [Children Act 1989, Section 31(1)]. This need to ensure there is effective control of children reflects the idea that children are at risk and so it is important parents are enabled, indeed required, to protect children.

Children must accept the wisdom of adults. One nine-year-old boy is quoted as saying:

> Adults like children when they behave and help with cleaning or tidying up and do what they are told, but not if they cry and shout and hit the adults – but sometimes also if they [children] say something funny. (Meyer 2007)

A sign of a mature child is that they have come to appreciate how little they know and will respect their elders and betters. So obedience is seen as a sign of maturity and disobedience a sign of immaturity. A child seeking to disagree with an adult cannot win. The mere fact of disobedience is indicative of immaturity.

This can be seen as most evident when looking at the ability of children to consent to medical treatment. If the child can demonstrate that they have *Gillick* (*Gillick v West Norfolk & Wisbech Area Health Authority* (1985) *UKHL* 7) competence (they are sufficiently mature to decide on the issue) they can give effective consent, but their refusal can be overridden. The implication being that where they are agreeing with the doctors that reassures us they do indeed have capacity, but where they disagree, then we doubt they really do have capacity.

3.3.2 The Quietening of Children

One of the consequences of the vulnerability description is that that children are declared to lack the capacity to be able to make decisions for themselves. Typically this is explained in terms of the poor decision making abilities: they lack the ability to comprehend the significance of facts; to project into the future; and suffer from an inability to focus on long-term goals, preferring short-term pleasures (Fortin 2009). These means that children lack sufficient capacity to make autonomous decisions.

The legal position is that while adults are presumed to have mental capacity to make decisions for themselves [Mental Capacity Act 2005, s.1(2)] no such presumption applies to children under the age of 16. The courts have acknowledged that children can be found to have sufficient capacity to make medical decisions (*Gillick* competence) and some other decisions (*Re Roddy* (2004) 1 FCR 481). However, even if Gillick competence they are still not in the same position as adults. For example their refusal to consent to treatment can be overridden if someone with parental responsibility or a court provides consent [Re W (A Minor) (1992) 3 WLR 758)] and a child under 16 cannot effectively consent to sexual intercourse (Sexual Offences Act 2003). One might rather conclude that a child's decision is respected if adults think they are making a good decision (Gilmore and Herring 2011)

Indeed, it is even worse than that. As children are not able to make their own decisions any views they have may reflect the views of adults, who use children to be mouth pieces. Hence Martin Guggenheim (2005, xii) writes that "children's rights' has become a mantra invoked by adults to help them in their own fights with other adults.' So not only is their decision making flawed, any views children do have may well not be theirs. A really good example of this is in cases of disputes over contact following parental separation. If a child says they do not want to see their father following separation, they are commonly seen as suffering from so-called 'alienation syndrome' through which one parent has turned the child's mind against the other. There is fierce dispute among family lawyers whether in fact this is merely a means by which a child's wishes can be discounted or whether it is proper appreciation of the pressure children are under. Certainly there have been some surprising cases where the views of the children have been seen as in the control of parents and children are not recognised (Re A (A Child) (2013) EWHC B 16). It should be remembered that adults are not forced to see people they do not want to see. Should children?

Munby P in *re H-B* (*Children*) (*Contact: Prohibitions on Further application*) (2015) EWCA Civ 389, para 76 certainly seemed to think so. In that case children were refusing to see their father and he expressed condemnation of the mother for failing to do more to persuade the children to see him:

I appreciate that parenting headstrong or strong-willed teenagers can be particularly taxing, sometimes very tough and exceptionally demanding. ... But parental responsibility does not shrivel away, merely because the child is 14 or even 16, nor does the parental obligation to take all reasonable steps to ensure that a child of that age does what it ought to be doing, and does not do what it ought not to be doing. I accept ....that a parent should not resort to brute force in exercising parental responsibility in relation to a fractious teenager. But what one can reasonably demand—not merely as a matter of law but also and much more fundamentally as a matter of natural parental obligation—is that the parent, by argument, persuasion, cajolement, blandishments, inducements, sanctions (for example, 'grounding' or the confiscation of mobile phones, computers or other electronic equipment) or threats falling short of brute force, or by a combination of them, does their level best to ensure compliance. That is what one would expect of a parent whose rebellious teenage child is foolishly refusing to do GCSEs or A-Levels or 'dropping out' into a life of drug-fuelled crime. Why should we expect any less of a parent whose rebellious teenage child is refusing to see her father?

However, in that case the father had not exactly behaved angelically. Further, a wide range of professionals had sought to encourage the girls to be positive about their father, and failed. Should a parent be expected to do what trained professionals cannot? Perhaps more importantly the case involved children aged 16 and 14. The analysis of the court seems unwilling to take seriously their own views of the matter and instead regards them as pawns in the hands of their parents. It is not possible that these young women have formed perfectly reasonable views of their own? Why should they not be listened to and respected? Is there not something rather patronising about suggesting the views of a 16 year old need to be changed by the mother by grounding her?

So children's views are given astonishingly little weight in court disputes, even when the dispute concerns the future of the child themselves. Despite some positive pronouncements in the Court of Appeal about the importance of involving children in litigation (*Mabon v Mabon* (2005) EWCA 634) the lack of finance to back this up reflects a failure to take children's involvement seriously (Fortin 2009). More significantly children are silenced through the pressure to encourage parents to resolve disputes themselves. Fortin (2009, 284) writes:

> the pressure imposed on separating parents to settle their disputes out of court often reinforces their children's isolation, ensuring that outsiders are kept totally unaware of their unhappiness and helplessness, with plans for their upbringing made over their heads.

It is most revealing, as Freeman (2001) notes, that the concerns over the involvement of children in litigation regarding their future family lives contrasts markedly with the willingness to prosecute children in the criminal courts. Children have sufficient capabilities to be punished for their decisions in criminal cases, but not sufficient capabilities for their decisions be given weight in family courts (Herring 2017).

3.3.3 *The Confinement of Children*

One of the most notable consequences of the vulnerability analysis of children is that children are limited in their freedoms. Children are seen as facing such risks that it is safest to keep children in their homes and away from public spaces and interacting with "strangers" (Appell 2009). Hearing that a child was regularly to be found at home would hardly be likely to create a social work investigation. Hearing a child was regularly found wandering the streets would. Typically children are seen to 'embody a state of innocence, purity and natural goodness that is only contaminated on contact with the corrupt outside world' (Kehily 2004, 5).

Restricting where children can go and their interactions with adults naturally follows from such a perception (Valentine 2000).

3.4 The Thinness of the Vulnerability Narrative

In this section I will seek to explore the thinness of the vulnerability narrative. My point will be that childhood is a time of vulnerability, but that by selecting only particular risks and particular kinds of children, an artificially narrow understanding of childhood is presented.

3.4.1 Selective

The vulnerability discourse is typically highly selective of the kinds of dangers that children face. Sexual abuse and physical harm at the hands of strangers tend to be emphasised. Yet the numbers of children who suffer sexual or physical abuse at the hands of strangers is tiny. Children are far more likely to be abused by someone known to them than a stranger. Far more children are harmed by the environment, social or economic harms. The 'vulnerability' used in the media presents the government as posing no risk to children: the risk is from individuals. The government is the protector children. Further, the risk is seen in terms that reinforce the protection offered by the traditional private family unit.

In the Independent newspaper (2014) there was an article on "Toxic Childhood". It claimed:

> Mental health risk to children trapped in "toxic climate" of dieting, pornography and school stress

This headline make the point well. We are worried about the risks of children and their eating habits, their pornography viewing and their stress. Yet adults suffer from precisely these same concerns.

3.4.2 Homogenisation

The vulnerability analysis also homogenises children. They are bounded together in their weakness, innocence and vulnerability. That fails to recognise either the diversity of children or of their childhood experiences. As Appell (2009, 750–751) describes:

> … this construction of childhood formulates the child as raceless (i.e., white) and middle-class, much like the raceless (i.e., white) middle-class man who is the liberal subject that feminist and critical theorists have exposed and contested. No matter who this child is

or from whence she or he comes, this same child is expected to become the white, male, middle-class, adult liberal subject upon reaching adulthood. Childhood's defining characteristics as natural, dependent, and private mask the differences among children while reinforcing the normative middle-class child as the measure of childhood; moreover, these characteristics further obfuscate the inequalities among the adult liberal subjects children are expected to become.

As must be obvious, the fears of the western parent that their children are at risk of obesity, overly-materialistic, or suffering low self-esteem have little resonance for those in the developing world (Morrow 2007). The western concern for children's vulnerability says little about the actual children, but much about the kind of society they live in and the worries of the adults.

3.4.3 Endangerment

A third reason to be sceptical about the use of vulnerability is that the vulnerability rhetoric can itself create dangers for the child. For example, to emphasise the horrors of child abuse, much is made of the sullying of the innocence of childhood. That is, however, a dangerous approach. As Kitzinger (2004) argues, it is this very kind of language of innocence and purity which plays a role in fuelling the paedophilic imagination. Further, she explains:

> Innocence, then, is a problematic concept because it is itself a sexual commodity and because a child who is anything less than 'an angel' may be seen as 'fair game', both by the courts and by other men who will avail themselves of a child they know has previously been abused. (Kitzinger 1988)

If the defiling of innocence is the mark of child abuse then where the child is not innocent, the abuse seems less. This should not be.

Referring back to a point made earlier, the vulnerability discourse encourages children to accept obedience and respect their parents and adults (Kitzinger 2004). Childhood compliance with adult demands and rules is deeply imbedded into our society's construction of childhood. Ironically, it is this which renders children so vulnerable in the arena of sexual contact (Kincaid 1998).

Rose (1989) argues:

> The modern child has become the focus of innumerable projects that purport to safeguard it from physical, sexual and moral danger, to ensure its 'normal' development, to actively promote certain capacities of attributes such as intelligence, education and emotional stability.

As Riney-Kehrberg (2005) puts it: childhood has moved indoors. Even when a child is outdoors, they are typically being supervised by adults and organised: "When a child is doing something (swimming in the public pool) it is usually sanctioned by adult authority and structured to be unresponsive to individual whims and fancies (no running or jumping in the pool)".

Kitzinger (1988) has argued how 'Childhood is presented as a time of play, an asexual and peaceful existence within the protective bosom of the family.' Yet this perception that public spaces are particularly dangerous for children might be questioned. Children are often more street-wise than adults (Scott 2000). Computers are seen as a source of sexual danger yet children are often more adept with the technology than adults. I can think of a whole host of areas about which my children are more knowledgeable and better equipped to navigate than I am.

3.5 Conclusion

Jackson and Scott write:

> [c]hildhood is increasingly being constructed as a precious realm under siege from those who would rob children of their childhoods, and as being subverted from within by children who refuse to remain childlike.

This chapter has explored how children are portrayed as vulnerable and the dangers in the vulnerability rhetoric in relation to children. There are dangers in particular in focused just on some dangers but not others; and by interventions that create further vulnerabilities, rather than finding solutions. As Brown (2015) argues "in a context of economic liberalism and welfare retrenchment, the rise of vulnerability in policy and practice can serve to further marginalise those who might be considered the 'most vulnerable'". However, to abandon it entirely and emphasise children's capabilities and resilience carries dangers too. I want to take a different tack.

References

Appell A (2009) The pre-political child of child-centered jurisprudence. Houston Law Review 46:703–765
Brown K (2015) Vulnerability and young people: care and social control in policy and practice. Policy Press, Bristol
Fortin J (2009) Children's rights and the developing law. Cambridge University Press
Freeman M (2001) The child in family law. In: Fiona J (ed) Legal concepts of childhood. Oxford University Press, Oxford
Gilmore S, Herring J (2011) No is the hardest word: consent and children's autonomy. Child and Family Law Quarterly 23:3–28
Guggeinheim M (2005) What's wrong with children's rights?. Harvard University Press, Cambridge Massachusetts
Herring J (2017) The age of criminal responsibility and the age of consent: Should they be any different? Northern Ireland Legal Quarterly 67:343–356
James A, Curtis P, Birch J (2008) Care and control in the construction of children's citizenship. In: Invernizzi A, Williams J (eds) Children and citizenship. Sage, London
Kaganas F, Diduck A (2004) Incomplete citizens: changing images of post-separation children. Modern Law Review 67:959–976

Kehily M (2004) An introduction to childhood studies. Open University Press, Buckingham
Kincaid J (1998) Erotic innocence: the culture of child molesting. Duke University Press, Durham
Kitzinger J (1988) Defending innocence: ideologies of childhood. Feminist Review 28:77–93
Kitzinger J (2004) Framing abuse: media influence and public understandings of sexual violence against children. Pluto Press, London
Meyer A (2007) The moral rhetoric of childhood. Childhood 14:85–101
Morrow V (2007) Editorial: at the crossroads. Childhood 14:5–8
Piper C (2008) Investing in children Willan. Cullompton
Riney-Kehrberg P (2005) Childhood on the farm: work, play, and coming of age in the Midwest. University of Kansas Press, Lawrence
Rose N (1989) Governing the soul. Free Association, London
Scott E (2000) Legal construction of adolescence. Hofstra Law Review 29:547–567
Taffel R, Blau M (1999) Nurturing good children now. St Martin's Press, New York
Valentine G (1996) Angels and devils: moral landscapes of childhood. Environment and Planning 14:581–602
Valentine G (2000) Children's geographies. Routledge, London

Chapter 4
Are Children More Vulnerable Than Adults?

Abstract Chapter 4 will challenge the assumption that children are more vulnerable than adults. It will explore the arguments in favour of universal vulnerability and argue that everyone (adults and children) has impaired capacity, is dependent on others, and has frail bodies. The argument will be made that childhood is a social construction created to disguise the vulnerability of adults. Rather than the more common argument that children's abilities are under-estimated and that they can be as competent as adults, it will be argued that adult's abilities are over-estimated and adults are as incompetent as children.

Keywords Vulnerability · Rationality · Values · Capacity · Bodies
Self · Identity

4.1 Introduction

As we have seen the argument that children are vulnerable and therefore in need of especial rights and protections is at the heart of the law's approach to children. Chapter 3 explored some of the negative consequences of portraying children as especially vulnerable. In this chapter I will challenge the assumption that children are more vulnerable than adults. At the heart of my claim will be the argument that everyone is vulnerable.

Vulnerability is an inherent human characteristic (Shildrick 2002). As Lévinas (1993, 123) states: 'The I, from head to foot and to the bone-marrow, is vulnerability.' Similarly Rogers et al. (2012, 12) write

> … all human life is conditioned by vulnerability, as a result of our embodied, finite, and socially contingent existence.

Of course, we adults prefer not to think of ourselves in this way. We highlight our independence, capacity for rational thought, maturity and autonomy. However, we puff ourselves up with such talk. The reality is very different. In fact, we are deeply dependent on others for our most basic needs; we are rarely in a position to make an informed decision and even when we do we are hardly rational; and though we like to imagine ourselves having autonomy and being author of our own lives, we have little control over ourselves (Redelmeier et al. 1993).

Part of our pretence to this idealised autonomous self is to claim that adults are completely different from adults. As Jenks (2005, 87) once perceptively stated:

> The child cannot be imagined without considering the idea of 'adult' just as it is impossible to picture the adult and society without positing 'the child.'

The categories and childhood are defined as a contrast. But this means that adults seek to deny their own vulnerability by projecting their vulnerabilities onto children. Day Sclater and Piper (2001, 409) explain:

> 'Projection' refers to an unconscious process whereby painful feelings are expelled from inside the self and located in another person. The subject can then deal with those feelings, as it were, at one step removed, as though they were characteristics of another. At its simplest, projection is happening when a part of the self is perceived in someone else, and we are therefore assisted, by a psychological defence mechanism, to avoid deeply painful emotions. It must be emphasized, however, that psychological mechanisms like projection are ordinary processes and are not indicative of pathology; projection is actually commonplace and ordinary.

They argue that, 'If adults can legitimately position children as vulnerable with reference to the welfare discourse, they may then have little incentive to confront the vulnerable feelings inside themselves.' They go on to argue:

> In a divorce situation, the welfare discourse both permits individuals to fight for the perceived needs of vulnerable children and allows children to become repositories for the overwhelming feelings of parents. It is difficult to avoid the conclusion that we, as adults, have an emotional investment in seeing things in the way that we do and in acting in the way that we do. Our analysis of the operation of the welfare principle in relation to divorce and separation would suggest that we are comfortable when regarding our children as vulnerable because this serves an emotional purpose for us. This, perhaps, is why achieving participation and autonomy rights for children is proving to be such a difficult thing to do (Day Sclater and Piper 2001, 413).

There is a strong analogy here to the response of able body people to disability. Shakespeare (2000) has suggested non-disabled people 'project their fear of death, their unease at their physicality and mortality onto disabled people, who represent all these difficult aspects of human existence.' It will be argued that adults do a similar thing with children.

4.2 Universal Vulnerability

The claim of universal vulnerability will be explored in this section. In the legal literature it has been championed by, in particular, the writing of Martha Fineman. She argues:

> The vulnerability approach recognizes that individuals are anchored at each end of their lives by dependency and the absence of capacity. Of course, between these ends, loss of capacity and dependence may also occur, temporarily for many and permanently for some

4.2 Universal Vulnerability

as a result of disability or illness. Constant and variable throughout life, individual vulnerability encompasses not only damage that has been done in the past and speculative harms of the distant future, but also the possibility of immediate harm. We are beings who live with the ever-present possibility that our needs and circumstances will change. On an individual level, the concept of vulnerability (unlike that of liberal autonomy) captures this present potential for each of us to become dependent based upon our persistent susceptibility to misfortune and catastrophe.

I would go further and question whether even in our 'prime' we do have the kind of autonomy and capacity traditional liberalism claims for adults.

Consider, for example, the work of Hurst (2008). In examining international guidelines of research ethics and setting out who might be regarded as vulnerable, she produces a list of vulnerable groups which include the following:

- Racial minorities
- The economically disadvantaged
- The very sick
- The institutionalized
- Children
- Prisoners
- Pregnant women and foetuses
- Incompetent persons
- Persons susceptible to coercion
- Persons who will not derive direct benefits from participation
- Persons for whom research is mixed with clinical care
- Junior or subordinate members of a hierarchical group ... [such as] medical and nursing students, subordinate hospital and laboratory personnel, employees of pharmaceutical companies, and members of the armed forces or police
- Elderly persons
- Residents of nursing homes
- Patients in emergency rooms
- Homeless persons
- Refugees or displaced persons
- Patients with incurable disease
- Individuals who are politically powerless
- Members of communities unfamiliar with modern medical concepts
- Patients with incurable diseases.

More factors could, no doubt, be added to this list (Coleman 2009). But notice, there must be few people who do not fall into one category or another. And her list is not unusual. The Declaration of Helsinki (World Medical Association 2008, A (9)) states that vulnerable groups include 'the economically and medically disadvantaged'; 'those who cannot give or refuse consent for themselves'; 'those who may be subject to giving consent under duress'; 'those who will not benefit personally from the research' and 'those for whom the research is combined with care.' Again the vast majority of the population could fit in with this description of vulnerability.

Consider these statistics. These are the kind of groups which are sometimes considered as "particularly vulnerable" and as can be seen they are so common as to question our norm of "non-vulnerability":

- 75% of the population have an IQ of less than 110 (Boeree 2009)
- There are over 11 million people with a limiting long term illness, impairment or disability in the UK (HM Government 2014).
- In any given week 1 in 6 people will experience some kind of mental health problem (McManus et al. 2016).
- In 2016, among those who had drink alcohol in England 27% were classed as binge drinkers in the week before being interviewed (Drinkaware 2017).
- In 2015, 58% of women and 68% of men were *overweight* or obese (NHS 2017).

My aim in citing such statistics is not to claim that the category of "vulnerable people" is larger than we commonly assume, but rather to argue that we are all vulnerable. I will expand that claim now.

Martha Fineman accepts that in a typical lifespan there will be times of different capacity and strengths. But, the typical 'adult liberal subject' focuses on just one part of that life span (middle age) and essentializes this as the standard. That means the vulnerable nature can get overlooked. Fineman (2013) argues:

> Throughout our lives we may be subject to external and internal negative, potentially devastating, events over which we have little control—disease, pandemics, environmental and climate deterioration, terrorism and crime, crumbling infrastructure, failing institutions, recession, corruption, decay, and decline. We are situated beings who live with the ever-present possibility of changing needs and circumstances in our individual and collective lives. We are also accumulative beings and have different qualities and quantities of resources with which to meet these needs of circumstances, both over the course of our lifetime and as measured at the time of crisis or opportunity.

The point here is that our nature is to be vulnerable. It is true that at different times and in different circumstances we may be more overtly in use of societal resources should not disguise the fact that we are in need of communal and relational support for all our lives (Daniel and Bowes 2011). We may be differently positioned within a web of economic and social relationships and this will impact on our experience of vulnerability and the resources at our disposal (Diduck 2013). Mackenzie et al. (2014) suggest that in addition to the inherent vulnerability that we all fact there is situational and pathogenic vulnerability. Situational vulnerability "may be caused or exacerbated by the personal, social, political, economic or environmental situation of individuals or social groups". Pathological vulnerability arise from abusive relationships or socio-political injustice. These other force interact with and on our universal vulnerability.

So, at different points our vulnerability may be more or less apparent and acute. As Fineman (2012) argues:

> Like vulnerability, dependency is universal: all of us have been dependent as infants and many will in the future become dependent on others for resources, care, and support. I am not talking about the idea of interdependence here, but about a physical or developmental aspect of the human condition. This form of dependence I have labelled 'inevitable.' All of us were dependent as children and many will become so as we age, fall ill, or become

disabled. This biological or developmental dependency is often thought of as the basis for denying agency or decision making autonomy to an individual and therefore is profoundly stigmatizing for adults and the basis for denying them, as well as children more generally, of certain liberties or rights. This embodied dependency has been assumed to attach to the elderly as a group, although many within that category are physically and mentally able.

I will now explore more precisely the source of this innate vulnerability we all have.

4.3 We Are All Dependent on Others

We might like to think we are self-sufficient and independent, but society has built up a wide range of structures and forms of assistance which disguise our vulnerability. We are profoundly dependent on others and social provision for survival. In a powerful article Lindemann (2003, 504) contrasts the emphasis that is paid to the "accommodations" that are put in place for disabled people, with the lack of appreciation of the accommodations for the able bodied:

> Colleagues, professional staff members, and other adults are unconscious of the numerous accommodations that society provides to make their work and life style possible. ATM's, extended hours in banks, shopping centres and medical offices, EZpass, newspaper kiosks, and elevators are all accommodations that make contemporary working life possible. There are entire industries devoted to accommodating the needs of adult working people. Fast food, office lunch delivery, day time child care, respite care, car washing, personal care attendants, interpreters, house cleaning, and yard and lawn services are all occupations that provide services that make it possible for adults to hold full time jobs.

So, while we highlight the "special accommodations" that are made for disabled people, we overlook the many accommodation that everyone needs to make their basic needs. No one can get up to the second floor of a building without an accommodation. You might needs stairs or you might need a lift, but we need something to assist us to get up there. Few people, if any, are able to meet their own food needs. Some need help putting the food into their moths, some need help in supermarkets bringing food to the door, some need food banks. But, we nearly all suffer from a need to rely on others to meet our most basic sustenance needs.

Neal (2012, 188) expands on why this reliance on others to meet our basic needs generates vulnerability:

> I am vulnerable because I am penetrable; I am permanently open and exposed to hurts and harms of various kinds. These two sources of vulnerability—reliance on others for co-operation, and openness to positive harm—are simply two means by which I might come to experience suffering; thus, it is suffering, and the capacity for suffering, that is definitive of this negative aspect of vulnerability. The extent and intensity of my vulnerability at a particular moment, or with regard to a particular need or harm, may be affected by my age, my sex, my degree of capacity, my health, my social status, my wealth, and a variety of other factors. Nevertheless, even the least vulnerable human being is still fundamentally, and inescapably, vulnerable in the negative sense, since none of us can meet her basic needs and satisfy her core desires without the co-operation of others; and even the most capable adult is vulnerable to hurt and harm, both physical and emotional.

Turning specifically to children, there are a mass of social structures, which are seen to legitimise and normalise the particular vulnerability of children. The fears of the "stranger danger"; the requirement for children (but not adults) to receive education; the "burdens of parenthood" (with no weight attached to the "burdens" of children caring for their parents) (Peterson and Wilkinson 2007). Children are, thereby, denied access to the resources adults require to appear independent, reinforcing the image of the vulnerable child and independent adult. The reality is that we are all, whether adult or child, deeply dependant on others for our well-being.

4.4 We All Have Impaired Capacity

It is commonly claimed that adults have better capacity to exercise autonomy than children. Indeed, that children generally, do not have the capacity to make the decision. That is commonly challenged by claiming that children are as capacitous as adults. For example, Gopnik et al. (2004), a developmental psychologist, reports even young children are as good as adults as theoretical reasoning. Indeed she event claims that babies "think, draw conclusions, make pre-dictions, look for explanations, and even do experiments". Such claims struggle to be fully convincing. As Matthews (1996) writes:

> For many people the art or philosophy of their childhood is never equaled, let alone surpassed, by the art or philosophy of their adult lives. If painting or doing philosophy has any non-instrumental value for them, it is their child art and their child philosophy that have such value.

Further, Gheaus (2018) argues that "it is not true that children are as bad at ends-means reasoning as they have been traditionally believed to be. Rather than a lack of rationality as such, it is their very limited experience of the world in combination with their lack of emotional self-control that justifies the view that children are insufficiently competent decision-makers and that they are subject to legitimate paternalism."

My claim will be that the presentation of adults being more capacitous than children involves an exacerbation about the abilities of adults, rather than under-appreciation of the abilities of children. As Welie and Welie (2001, 125) suggest:

> the autonomous patient – or, more precisely, the patient who invokes his right to respect his autonomy in order to exert his freedom and personal responsibility – is the exception rather than the rule. The incompetent patient is the rule, the starting point – or, more precisely, the patient in the care of whom concerns about autonomy (in the libertarian sense of that term) do not even arise. …The question, then, is not when does a patient become incompetent, but what makes him competent such that his call for respect of his autonomy must be granted, notwithstanding risk to well-being, health or life.

Similarly Clough (2017) notes that

> Whilst it may be presented that we are all free and unencumbered, it is inescapable that we are all impacted upon and shaped by social structures, institutions and discourses. What is important, then, is thinking about how these structures are working, and how they are

impacting upon particular experiences. The critical point here is that when the focus is shifted to the interaction of various sources of vulnerability, we can thus hone in on how responses can best be framed to facilitate autonomy in a thicker and more meaningful sense, which may involve access to particular resources, or supports in making decisions.

To appreciate these claims we need to explore what it means to have capacity.

The standard model of capacity is that P must understand the relevant information, and be able to use the information to make a decision. As section 3 of the Mental Capacity Act 2005 puts it:

A person is unable to make a decision for himself if he is unable—

(a) to understand the information relevant to the decision,
(b) to retain that information,
(c) to use or weigh that information as part of the process of making the decision, or
(d) to communicate his decision (whether by talking, using sign language or any other means).

Wall (2017) suggests from a philosophical point of view that in order to be able to act autonomously a person ought to be able:

1. to act free from undue influence or influence of others (the freedom condition)
2. to exercise the capacity for rational thought and cognition (the competence condition) and
3. to act according to the beliefs, values and commitments the persons identifies or endorses as their own beliefs, values and commitments (the authenticity question)

Let us explore these elements a little further and see if the claim that adults can be presumed to have capacity less than children stacks up.

4.4.1 Information

In respect of any complex decision. Adults are rarely familiar with the key facts. That is why we seek the advice of professionals and others. Consider, for example, the question of consent to delivery of a baby. Cobb J. recently held *The Mental Health Trust v DD* [2014] EWCOP 11 at [65]:

> In considering the mode of the delivery of the baby, I suggest that a prospective mother would need to be able to understand, retain and weigh the information relevant to:
>
> (i) Ante-natal care and monitoring, including blood tests to check for anaemia and diabetes; urine tests to check for infections; the benefits of discussion with health services about delivery options;
> (ii) Ante-natal monitoring of the foetus; the value of an ultra-sound imaging;
> (iii) Mode of delivery of the baby, including vaginal delivery, and caesarean section;

(iv) Natural and/or induced labour;
(v) Anaesthesia and pain relief;
(vi) The place of delivery—e.g. at home or in a hospital—and the risks and benefits of each option;
(vii) The risk of complications, arising from conditions relevant to the mother or the baby;
(viii) Post-natal care of mother and baby.

It is hard to believe that more than a tiny of the population could be taken to know this information.

Of course, that is but one example, but in order to fully appreciate the significance of the fact we need to be aware of the consequence of our actions and where we will be as a result of them. Our choice typically can be no more than guesswork. In the vast majority of important decisions that we make, where we are doing more than just expressing a personal preference and our understanding of the facts is very limited.

There is now an extensive literature (helpfully summarised in Conly 2014) demonstrating the wide range of cognitive biases, errors in perceptions and failures in understanding that contribute to our bad decisions. We simply, in many cases, lack the time, knowledge, insight and foreknowledge, to know anything like enough information to be richly capacitous.

4.4.2 Rationality

To be autonomous a person must not only understand the information they must be able to use it. Drobac and Goodenough (2015), in their analysis of the psychology of decision making, list the following requirements for rational use of information:

(i) parties with stable, well ordered preferences,
(ii) choices that are fully voluntary and unconstrained;
(iii) relatively equal, and ideally complete, information;
(iv) relatively equal bargaining power and experience;
(v) sufficient cognitive capacity to evaluate the transaction and to exercise voluntary control over the conflicting factors and emotions involved;
(vi) the absence of monopoly power or other distortions of the market,
(vii) the presence of good faith and absence of fraud in both parties; and
(viii) a level of consequence for a mistake that is not disastrous to the party.

The authors, after examining the latest neuroscience and psychology suggest that few people have capacity. Similarly, Levy (2014) refers to a wide range of psychological studies which reveal 'fallibilities of human reasoning' (including 'myopia for the future', 'motivated reasoning' and 'biases' in 'assessing probabilities… exacerbated… under cognitive load'). He concludes that 'Human beings are, under a variety of conditions, systematically bad reasoners, and many of their reasoning faults can be expected to affect the kind of judgements that they make when they are called upon to give informed consent'. Further, effect Conly (2014) writes:

> As has by now been discussed convincingly and exhaustively (notably by Nobel Prize-winning Daniel Kahneman and Amos Tversky), we suffer from common, apparently ineradicable tendencies to 'cognitive bias,' which means that in many common situations, our decision-making goes askew. These biases are many and varied, but they have in common that they interfere with our appreciation of even quite simple facts, and lead us to choose ineffective means to our ends.

As all these authors show adults are arbitrary, irrational, biased and confused in their decision making ability.

4.4.3 Values

To have autonomy it is necessary for a person to have values and relate the information to their goals (Herring and Wall 2015). Mackenzie and Rogers (2013) argue that to be able to exercise autonomy people need to be the following:

- self-determining: being "able to determine one's own beliefs, values, goals and wants, and to make choices regarding matters of practical import to one's life free from undue interference. The obverse of self-determination is determination by other persons, or by external forces or constraints."
- Self-governing: "being be able to make choices and enact decisions that express, or are consistent with, one's values, beliefs and commitments. Whereas the threats to self-determination are typically external, the threats to self-governance are typically internal, and often involve volitional or cognitive failings. Weakness of will and failures of self-control are common volitional failings that interfere with self-governance"
- Having authenticity: "a person's decisions, values, beliefs and commitments must be her 'own' in some relevant sense; that is, she must identify herself with them and they must cohere with her 'practical identity', her sense of who she is and what matters to her. Actions or decisions that a person feels were foisted on her, which do not cohere with her sense of herself, or from which she feels alienated, are not autonomous."

Again it must be questioned how many people can claim to satisfy these kinds of requirements. We are all heavily influenced by our social and family environment.

So the assumptions that adults have capacity and are able to exercise autonomy must be questioned. Children are no doubt impaired in decision making capacity but so are adults. Both adults and children make decisions based on inadequate information, irrationally, using values which they have not been free to adopt.

I am not arguing that people's decisions do not deserve respect but the basis of that should not be autonomy. Our decisions are not the result of applying our selected values to sound understanding of the facts in a rational way. Our decision making is impulsive, sometimes short-termist, biased and incoherent. That is so for adults and children.

4.4.4 The Exaggerated Significance of Capacity

It might be thought that what I am promoting is some kind of paternalistic hell where we are deemed to lack capacity to make any decisions for ourselves and all decisions are made by the state. However, that is not my argument. Indeed the points I am making is that any decision maker (be it judge, politician or doctor) will suffer from these impaired decision-making.

So my argument is rather that we should not be seeking to justify respect for decision making based on autonomy or capacity, but rather claims such as respect for liberty, promotion of diversity, or dignity (See Herring 2009 for further development).

Part of what is behind the distinction drawn between children and adults is therefore an improper elevation of rational thought as being the key marker of moral personhood. We can see this in its most extreme with those who question whether those with severe mental disability should or should not be regarded as moral people (Singer 2009). Similarly, children are seen as *potential* citizens, and as regarded as having 'the right to a free future' (Mills 2003). Children are not there yet, but are on their way.

Feder Kittay (2005, 95) has written movingly of the attitudes displayed towards her severely disabled daughter, Sesha:

> Sesha's life is a human life, but a tragic one be-cause her situation is such that she can never achieve functioning of all the capabilities to some satisfactory degree. I believe that were Sesha capable of replying, she would remind us that people with disabilities have worked hard to insist that life with impairments, even serious impairments need not be 'tragic'. What is tragic is the failure of the larger society to include people with variant bodies and modes of functioning. Yes, when Sesha was born I had envisioned a different future for her. Yes, when I learned of her very significant impairments I saw a human tragedy. But I have since learned — from her, from the disability community and from my own observations — that she is capable of having a very good life, one full of joy, of love, of laughter: a life that includes the appreciation of some of the best of human culture, great music and fine food, and the delights of nature, water, the scent of flowers, the singing of birds. No, she cannot participate in political life, she cannot marry and have children, she cannot read a book or engage in moral reasoning, but her life is richly human and full of dignity. We need to work hard to see that her life is not tragic …

Feder Kittay in this passage shows how the disabled can be branded and defined by their lack of abilities in accordance with the norm. Yet, her emphasis is on Sesha's capabilities. We could make similar points about children. If we value in humanity not, or not only, a certain kind of rational thought, but the capacity for wonder, for unconditional loving, intense feeling, then many children have these to a greater extent than many adults.

Feder Kittay (2005, 97) concludes her discussion of dignity with a central point:

> I urge that we not look for the basis of dignity in attributions we have as individuals, but in the relationships we bear to one another. Relationships of caring serve as conduits of worth — the worth of the caregiver is conferred on the one to whom she devotes herself.

This raises another important point about our autonomy and that is we rarely make our decisions alone. We make them together with others. We realise the impact of decisions rarely impacts just those who making them. Our decisions are made in and through our relationships. Indeed, in relationships of care it is hard to separate out who is the cared for and who is carer (Herring 2008). Children often rely on adults to help them produce decisions which are made jointly. The same is true for adults too.

So, in all the ways discussed in this section, adults exhibit the lack of understanding, lack of rationality, bias and need for support, that children are said to exhibit in their decision-making. This does not provide a basis of treating children and adults differently.

4.5 The Vulnerability of the Human Body

Another difference that is commonly relied upon to distinguish adults and children is the weakness and smallness of a child's body compared with an adults. However, this is also faced on a false image of the security around the adult body. In fact our corporality creates vulnerability.

Our bodies are vulnerable to sickness, illness, and accidents (Matambanadzo 2012). Our health is frail. As Fineman (2013) puts it: '[W]e are born, live, and die within a fragile materiality that renders all of us constantly susceptible to destructive external forces and internal disintegration?' Our bodies programmed to wear down and tire (Carse 2006). Death itself is the ultimate sign of that.

Our bodies are 'profoundly leaky' (Shildrick 1997). They are constantly changing with new material being added to them and old material being discarded. Inside our bodies we are dependent on a wide range of non-human material to survive and outside it is constantly interacting with the environment (Chau and Herring 2007).

We should notice however, that these vulnerabilities affect not only us, but also those we are in relationships with. Not only are we at risk of harm to our own bodies, the bodies of those we are in relationships are at risk of harm, and injuries to their bodies can impact on ours.

We are in our nature embodied people. Academics are, perhaps, particularly prone to elevate the cerebral above the physical, but there is no denying that the frailty of our bodies catches up with us all. We hide the vulnerabilities created by our bodies by emphasizing the enclosed, controlled, bounded body (Perpich 2010). This is most powerfully reflected, I would argue, in the claim that we own our bodies (Herring 2014). The truth is our bodies are in constant flux; profoundly leaky; deeply dependant on other bodies and the broader environment (Neal 2012).

4.6 The Vulnerable Self

Another distinguishing feature of childhood and adulthood which is commonly relied upon is that children's identities and social resources are more limited than adults. However, this too overplays the independence of adults. In a radical sense people's relationships constitute their selves (Gergen 2009; McLaughlin 2012). This is even more radical than it might at first sound. It is not that we have selves that join together to form relationships, but it is out of our relationships that the self exists. We primarily understand our selves in terms of how we related to others and our social interactions. From our beginnings, the words we use and understanding of the world comes from our interactions with our carers. This understanding of the self means we are constant danger of our self being challenged by others rejecting us; not accepting us as members of a group; not providing the support we expect; or using our relationships to harm us.

This means explains why we are all vulnerable in our sense of self. If people are constituted through their relationships with others, then we are dependent on others and our trust is given to them (Baier 1994). That makes the self inherently vulnerable. Butler (2004, 20) explains why: 'Loss and vulnerability seem to follow from our being socially constituted bodies, attached to others, at risk of losing those attachments, exposed to others, at risk of violence by virtue of that exposure.'

4.7 Care

Another difference that is commonly emphasised between adults and children is that adults require care and are dependent on others, while adults are not. However, I argue dependency is an inevitable facet of human life (Herring 2013). It is true there may be times in life when we are more in need of care than others However, often then others will be dependent on us to meet their needs, be that as parents or carers for others. This itself creates a vulnerability (Dodds 2014). Our responsibilities to meet the needs of others in one sense limits our lives. We are on constant call to meet others. Their vulnerabilities become a feature of the relationship. Feder Kittay (1999, xii) wrote of our interdependence:

> My point is that this interdependence begins with dependence. It begins with the dependency of an infant, and often ends with the dependency of a very ill or frail person close to dying. The infant may develop into a person who can reciprocate, an individual upon whom another can be dependent and whose continuing needs make her interdependent with others. The frail elderly person ... may herself have been involved in a series of interdependent relations. But at some point there is a dependency that is not yet or no longer an interdependency. By excluding this dependency from social and political concerns, we have been able to fashion the pretense that we are independent—that the cooperation between persons that some insist is interdependence is simply the mutual (often voluntary) cooperation between essentially independent persons.

4.7 Care

As Williams (2002, 503) argues we need to recognize 'us all as interdependent and as having the potential and responsibility to be caring and cared for'. If care is an essential part of what it is to be person and care produces vulnerability then vulnerability is an essential part of being a person. There is a false distinction drawn between children being dependant on adults, and adults not being dependent on children.

Indeed one of the ironies of the vulnerability of children discourse is that it has become a source of vulnerability for adults. Every parent knows the sinking stomach when the child is not in the place you expected her to be (Kehily 2010). Parenthood is in danger of becoming a time of near constant fear. Increasingly parenthood is seen as a time of great pressure. As Beck-Gersheim (1996, 48) puts it:

> A child can no longer be accepted as it is, with physical idiosyncrasies, perhaps even flaws. Rather, it becomes the target of a diversity of efforts. All possible flaws must be corrected… all possible talents must be stimulated…Countless guides to education and upbringing appear on the book and magazine market. As different as each one is, at bottom they all have a similar message: the success of the child is defined as the private duty and responsibility of the parents/the mother. And the duty reads the same everywhere: the parents must do everything to give the child 'the best start in life.'

The requirements or expectations on parents are excessive. Furedi (2014) focuses on the role of experts and the 'scientification of child rearing' in relation to parents and their ability to take personal responsibility regarding their children:

> Contemporary parenting culture exhorts parents to bring up their children according to 'best practice.' In virtually every area of social life today, experts advocate the importance of seeking help. Getting advice – and, more importantly, following the script that has been authored by experts – is seen as proof of 'responsible parenting.'

Parenthood has become a matter for experts, or at least 'supernanny'. Parents need special skills and training to do the job. This, however, can set up parents to fail.

Worse it presents parenthood as a job. Parenting has become a skill set to be learned, rather than a relationship to be lived. Children are presented as the passive recipients of parenthood. Yet, parent-child relationships are not like that. Children 'parent' the adults as much as adults parent children. Children care, mold, control, discipline, cajole their parents; just as parents do the same for children. One of the great wrongs of a parent is to seek to hyper-parent a child in a way that seeks to impose a particular view of what is a good life on their child, although that is wrong. It is the wrong of failing to be open to change as an adult; failing to learn from children, failing to see that the things you thought were important are, in fact, not. It is failing to find the wonder, fear, loneliness, anxiety, spontaneity and joy of children and to re-find them for oneself (see Herring 2017). So our image of parenting with is binary division into parent and child misleads us in dangerous ways in understanding the mutuality of the relationships, marked by care, support and discovery.

4.8 Are Children Special?

Dixon and Nussbaum (2012) rely on the capabilities approach to make an argument that there should be "special propriety" to children's rights, as compared with adult's rights. They start by arguing that "children's rights should be recognized as human rights, because every human being, under this approach, is entitled to respect for her full human dignity." They then go on to provide two arguments for when "special priority" should be given to children's rights. First, "where children are especially vulnerable as a result of their legal and economic dependence on adults, as well as their inherent physical or emotional vulnerability". Second, "where the marginal cost of protecting children's rights is either so low that denying such a right would be a direct affront to their dignity, or where it is far more cost-effective to protect that right than an equivalent right for adults". It is worth exploring these claims further.

As to the first point, they explain that at the heart of a capabilities approach is an assessment of people's real opportunity for functioning and choice. This is important for each and every individual. That includes children. Nussbaum and Dixon explain that agency has a central role to play in capabilities approach. This concerns not only the "satisfaction of preferences", but also "the growth of agency and practical reason". To them this means "that children should be afforded the maximum scope for decisional, freedom consistent with their actual-or potential capacity for rational and reasoned forms of choice, or judgment." This, they accept could mean that an adolescent would have rights to sexual and reproductive matters or religious choices. Even younger children should have the right to make certain decisions as that "provides an important opportunity to practice thinking, and making decisions, within certain protected bounds, so as to develop their future capacity for meaningful agency." Of course, such a point could readily be made in relational to adults. So the important point for this book is there argument that children differ from adults in "the support they require from the state, in order to develop and enjoy their capabilities." In short, here the point is that adults do not require assistance from the state to enjoy their capabilities. The problem, as Nussbaum and Dixon, acknowledge is that adults with cognitive disability do. The question then arises whether the difference in claim reflects not a point to do with age, but rather with capacity to enjoy capabilities. They acknowledge the "clear points of analogy" between children and adults with cognitive disabilities, but do not explain the difference. The do emphasise that children are "profoundly dependent on adults for a substantial time" and that physical, emotional and choice making abilities only arrive in late adolescence. But that same point could be made with those with cognitive impairments. Similarly their argument that:

> children are completely dependent on the care of others. Furthermore, their immobility means that, even though their cognition can develop rapidly, they remain at the mercy of their surroundings for cognitive and emotional stimulation and stability.

4.8 Are Children Special?

It seems, therefore, at best Dixon and Nussbaum make a case for saying although everyone needs support of some kind to realise their capabilities, there are some people who need more support than others. Children may be prominent among that group, but it consists of people who are not children and there are children who are not in that group. Most importantly the distinguishing feature of that group is not being a child, but lacking the capacity to develop and enjoy their capabilities. They further downplay the support every human needs to realise their capabilities.

A slightly different argument they use is that even if we say children have the same rights as others it may be that difference resources are needed to give effect to their rights. For example:

> children's imagination and creativity, for example, are likely to be stimulated by quite different books than those that appeal to adults; and children are also likely to experience quite different levels of trauma, and psychological harm, as a result of experiences such as detention.

Again, while it may be true that the material which will stimulate some people and not others, it is far from clear whether this can be put down to age per se. The Harry Potter books may have more readers under sixteen than over, but there are plenty of people over 16 who greatly enjoy these and plenty under sixteen who do not. It is not clear, save in a very generalised way, that age is the material factor here. In short as Dixon and Nussbuam acknowledge "it is also important to recognize that many forms of vulnerability experienced by children are common to others-including adults with cognitive disabilities."

So might any difference be found? One might be the argument, mentioned by Dixon and Nussbaum, that making decisions for a young child would be normal and expected, but in relational to an adult with impaired capacity we would wish to avoid infatuation. This, however, is unclear. Parents often attempt to negotiate with children and encourage children to reach the "right" conclusion through their own thought. It is not clear that the method of discourse is that different from carers of adults with cognitive disabilities. Further it may well be that Dixon and Nussbuam in explaining it is normal and expected for adults to make decisions for children are doing no more than state the current assumptions about childhood, rather than justify them.

Gheaus (2018) makes a different argument and refers to some goods that she believes are unique to childhood: "engaging in world discovery, artistic creation, philosophical pursuits and experimentation with one's self." These, she argues, can only be fully access during childhood. For it is only in childhood that our self is not yet set and we can experiment with who we are and what we can be. We can try new ways of seeing and interacting with the world, before "becoming set in our ways" in adulthood. She explains further:

> the experiencing of caring affection from adults whom the children can trust and love wholeheartedly and unstructured time during which children engage in fantasy play, experimentation and undirected exploration of the world and of their minds.

It is true that some people are very "stuck in their ways" and some that are open to change and experimentation, but it is far from clear that tracks the adulthood/childhood distinction. Indeed often in childhood people simply reflect the attitudes, beliefs and interests of their parents. Similarly adulthood for some can be a time of constant remaining of the self. So, again, there seems no particular reason to restrict these goods to childhood.

A similar response can be made in relation to other arguments. Harry Brighouse and Adam Swift argue that an "innocence about sexuality" and being carefree are goods of childhood. But it is far from clear that these characteristics are unique to childhood. Some children are sexually innocent, some are not; similarly with adults. Intoxicated people are often carefree (Hannah 2017) and there are plenty of reports of childhood being a time of stress.

4.9 The Social Construction of Childhood

Todres (2014) summarises well the popular image of childhood:

> the dominant view of children today is that they are adults in the making—that is, dependent individuals who are not yet capable of mature and autonomous thought or action and who need to be socialized to conform to the world.

This perceived childhood as a time of development: a shift from incapacity to capacity; from dependence to self-sufficiency; from childhood to adulthood. However, in this chapter, it will argued that is a false understanding of humanity.

The argument here is, therefore, that childhood is a social construction. There is no natural state of "childhood" at which people then move to another state of adulthood, with some significant difference between the two. Rather society assumes that childhood is a particular set of experiences and labels these as childhood and attaches a particular meaning to these. The fact that that meaning varies between cultures and societies and at different times, show that the meaning of childhood is not a natural given, but reflects the attitudes of the broader society. Norozi and Moen (2016) write

> The idea that childhood is socially constructed refers to the understanding that childhood is not natural process rather it is society which decides when a child is a child and when a child becomes an adult.
>
> The notion of childhood cannot be seen in isolation. It is deeply intertwined with other factors in society.

Indeed it is striking that, as noted in Chap. 1, defining childhood has become problematic. Norozi and Moen (2016) in attempting to define the unifying concept suggest: "childhood is considered as the early phase of the human life." But that does not get us very far as it does not define what the "early phrase" means. It might used to a physical size or development or mental developments. It may be easier to contrast to adulthood. It is "non-adulthood" and perhaps that is reflected in the way that infirm old age is commonly regarded as "a second childhood". As Woodhead (2013) states "children are constructed as not yet adult, as in process of 'becoming' rather than a person in their own right". James et al. (1998) suggest that the childhood is seen as "imperfection" and dependency, a route to the independency and perfection of adulthood. In this sense childhood is understood to be the absence of a characteristic:

> The understanding of childhood, the view of children, is very much an "adult" projection; we often unconsciously see them as what we are not, as what we fear and what we miss (Mouritsen 2002, 34)

It might seem that the most natural understanding of childhood is that it relates to age. So, the United Nations Convention on the Rights of Child (UNCRC) anyone below the age of eighteen is prospected as a child. This, however, is problematic. There seems a huge difference between those who are six months old and those who are seventeen, indeed more significant than between those who are seventeen and those who are thirty. If all that unites this group is that they have a chronological age, that does not suggest that anything particularly meaningful can be said.

Even if we were to replace age with certain physical, social and psychological developments, this would not capture what is commonly understood by age. These are acquired at different ages by different people and often depend significantly on social, education and cultural contexts. It would also depend enormously on what counted as being the developmental milestones seen as significant. For example, we might choose how well one can operate a mobile phone or how well one can run 10 km or comfort a person in distress. It is unlikely capacities in these areas necessarily relate to age. We would be rapidly returning to the argument that this is simply a social construction. Aries (1982) claims that in medieval society that a child was an adult as soon as she could live without the continuous care of others. Her augment has been criticised (Gittens 2004), but clearly the age of marriage and so forth has change. Certainly our understanding of child abuse and the dangers to childhood has challenged the assumptions about childhood. So much of what we think we know about childhood is subject to assumptions that are made, often idealised ones, rather than being based in any scientific facts about the inevitable nature of childhood.

4.10 Conclusion

Many of the common arguments around the differences between children and adults are based on a view of childhood as deficient (Kane 2015). Arneil (2002, 88) argues that we need to stop viewing the child as a "becoming" and instead as a "being"— that is, as the child is *now,* and not in relation to a future self. The child is currently a valuable person and is subject to many of the foibles, weaknesses and inconsistencies of adulthood.

This chapter has sought to argue that adults show precisely the same vulnerabilities that children do. Of course, we do differ in our capacities, our openness and attitudes, these differences are marked more by our socio-economic background, education and class than whether we are children or adults. Both childhood and adulthood is marked as times of profound vulnerability, interdependence and incapacity. It is adult's refusal to acknowledge their childish natures that creates the false impression that a sharp line needs to be drawn between the young and the old.

References

Aries P (1982) The discovery of childhood. In: Jenks C (ed) The sociology of childhood. Essential readings. Batsford, London
Arneil B (2002) Becoming versus being. In: MacLeon C, Archard D(eds) The moral and political status of children. Oxford University Press, Oxford
Baier A (1994) Moral prejudices: essays on ethics. Harvard University Press, Cambridge
Beck-Gersheim E (1996) Individualization and 'precarious freedoms': perspectives and controversies of a subject-orientated sociology. In Heelas P, Lash S, Morris P (eds) Detraditionalisation. Blackwell Publishers, Oxford
Boeree G (2009) Intelligence and IQ at http://webspace.ship.edu/cgboer/intelligence.html
Butler J (2004) Precarious life. Verso, London
Carse A (2006) Vulnerability, agency and human flourishing. In Taylor C, Dell'Oro R (eds) Health and human flourishing. Georgetown University Press, Washington
Chau P-L, Herring J (2007) My body, your body, our bodies. Med Law Rev 15:34–56
Clough B (2017) Disability and vulnerability: challenging the capacity/incapacity binary. Soc Policy Soc 16:469–481
Coleman C (2009) Vulnerability as a regulatory category in human subject research. J Law Med Ethics 7:12–31
Conly S (2014) Against autonomy. J Med Ethics 40:349–353
Daniel B, Bowes A (2011) Re-thinking harm and abuse: insights from a lifespan perspective. Br J Soc Work 41:820–836
Day Sclater S, Piper C (2001) Social exclusion and the welfare of the child. J Law Soc 29:409–425
Diduck A (2013) Autonomy and vulnerability in family law: the missing link. In: Wallbank J, Herring J (eds) Vulnerabilities, care and family law. Routledge, Abingdon
Dixon R, Nussbaum M (2012) Children's rights and a capabilities approach: the question of special priority. Cornell Law Rev 97:549
Dodds S (2014) Dependence, care and vulnerability. In: Mackenzie C, Rogers W, Dodds S (eds) Vulnerability: new essays in ethics and feminist philosophy. Oxford University Press, Oxford
Drink Aware (2017) Consumption. Drinkaware, London
Drobac J, Goodenough O (2015) Exposing the myth of consent. Indiana Health Law Rev 12:471–521
Feder Kittay E (1999) Love's labor: essays on women, equality and dependency. Routledge, New York
Feder Kittay E (2005) Equality, dignity and disability. In: Lyons MA, Waldron F (eds) Perspectives on equality. Liffey Press, Dublin
Fineman M (2012) "Elderly" as vulnerable: rethinking the nature of individual and societal responsibility. Elder Law Rev 17:23–65
Fineman M (2013) Feminism, masculinities and multiple identities. Nevada Law Rev 13:619–654

References

Furedi F (2014) Forward. In: Lee E, Birstow J, Fairclouth C, Macvarish J (eds) Parenting Culture Studies. Palgrave, Basingstoke

Gergen K (2009) Relational being. Oxford University Press, Oxford

Gheaus A (2018) Children's vulnerability and legitimate authority over children. J Appl Philos 35 (S1):60–75

Gittens D (2004) The historical construction of childhood. In: Kehily M (ed) An introduction to childhood studies. Open University Press, Buckingham

Gopnik A, Glymour C, Sobel D, Schulz L, Kushnir T, Danks D (2004) A theory of causal learning in children: causal maps and bayes nets. Psychol Rev 111:3–32

Hannah S (2017) Why childhood is bad for children. J Appl Philos 1–18

Herring J (2008) Caregivers in medical law and ethics. J Contemp Health Law Policy 25:1–34

Herring J (2009) Losing it? Losing what? The law and dementia. Child Fam Law Q 21:3–29

Herring J (2013) Caring and the law. Hart, Oxford

Herring J (2014) Why we need a statute regime to regulate bodily material. In: Goold I, Herring J, Skene L, Greasley K (eds) Persons, parts and property: how should we regulate human tissue in the 21st century?. Hart Publishing, Oxford

Herring J (2017) Parental responsibility, hyper-parenting and the role of technology. In: Brownsword R, Scotford E, Yeung K (eds) The oxford handbook of law, regulation and technology. Routledge, Abingdon

Herring J, Wall J (2015) Autonomy, capacity and vulnerable adults: filling the gaps in the Mental Capacity Act. Legal Stud 35(4):698–719

HM Government (2014) Disability facts and figures. HM Government, London

Hurst S (2008) Vulnerability in research and health care. Bioethics 22:187–203

James A, Jenks C, Prout A (1998) Childhood in social space. In: James A, Chris J, Prout A (eds) Theorizing childhood. Sage, London

Jenks C (2005) Childhood projection. Routledge, London

Kane L (2015) Childhood, growth and dependency in liberal political philosophy. Hypatia 31:156–170

Kehily M (2010) Childhood in crisis? Tracing the contours of 'crisis' and its impact upon contemporary parenting practices. Media Cult Soc 32:171–185

Lévinas E (1993) Humanismo Del Otro Hombre. Caparros, Madrid

Levy N (2014) Forced to be free? Increasing patient autonomy by constraining it. J Med Ethics 40:293–298

Lindemann K (2003) The ethics of receiving. Theor Med Bioeth 24:501–524

Mackenzie C, Rogers W (2013) Autonomy, vulnerability and capacity: a philosophical appraisal of the Mental Capacity Act. Int J Law Context 9:37–61

Mackenzie C, Rogers W, Dodds S (2014) Vulnerability. New essays in ethics and feminist philosophy. Oxford University Press, Oxford

Matambanadzo S (2012) Embodying vulnerability: a feminist theory of the person. Duke J Gend Law Policy 20:45–98

Matthews G (1996) The philosophy of childhood. Harvard University Press, Cambridge, MA

McLaughlin K (2012) Surviving identity: vulnerability and the psychology of recognition. Routledge, Abingdon

McManus S, Bebbington P, Jenkins R, Brugha T (eds) (2016) Mental health and wellbeing in England: adult psychiatric morbidity survey. NHS Digital, London

Mills C (2003) The child's right to an open future. J Soc Philos 34:499–521

Mouritsen F (2002) Child culture-play culture. In: Mouritsen F, Qvortrup J (eds) Childhood and children's culture. University Press of Southern Denmark, Odense

Neal M (2012) "Not gods but animals": human dignity and vulnerable subjecthood. Liverpool Law Rev 33:177–198

NHS (2017) Obesity. NHS, London

Norozi S, Moen T (2016) Childhood as a social construction. J Educ Soc Res 6:75–92

Perpich D (2010) Vulnerability and the ethics of facial tissue transplantation. Bioethical Inq 7: 173–198

Peterson A, Wilkinson I (2007) Health, risk and vulnerability. Routledge, Abingdon
Redelmeier D, Rozin P, Kahneman D (1993) Understanding patients' decisions: cognitive and emotional perspectives. J Am Med Assoc 270:72–98
Rogers W, Mackenzie C, Dodds S (2012) Why bioethics needs a theory of vulnerability. Int J Feminist Approaches Bioeth 5:11–25
Shakespeare T (2000) Help. Verso, London
Shildrick M (1997) Leaky bodies and boundaries. Routledge, Abingdon
Shildrick M (2002) Embodying the monster: encounters with the vulnerable self. Routledge, London
Singer P (2009) Speciesism and moral status. Metaphilosophy 40:56–82
Todres J (2014) Independent children and the legal construction of childhood. South Calif Interdisc Law J 23:261–304
Wall J (2017) Being oneself. In: Foster C, Herring J (eds) Depression and the law. Oxford University Press, Oxford
Welie J, Welie S (2001) Is incompetence the exception or the rule? Med Health Care Philos 4: 125–141
Williams F (2002) The presence of feminism in the future of welfare. Econ Soc 31:502–526
Woodhead M (2013) Childhood: a developmental approach. In: Kehily M (ed) Understanding childhood: a cross disciplinary approach. The Open University, Buckingham
World Medical Association (2008) Declaration of Helsinki

Chapter 5
Childhood, Adulthood and the Law

Abstract This chapter will explore the consequence of accepting that adults are as vulnerable as children. It will argue this requires a rethinking of the nature of legal rights and responsibilities. The law needs to promote values of relationships and mutuality, rather than individualism and autonomy. It will also require a different response to vulnerability. Rather than seeing vulnerability as a state to be avoided or to escape from it will require the law to recognise our vulnerabilities and the responsibilities we owe to each other as a result.

Keywords Rights · Vulnerability · Care · Age of consent · Responsibilities
Public/private

5.1 Introduction

So far, this book has explored the common assumption that children are more vulnerable than adult to a range of risks and harms and so they deserve a special status in the law. I have explored the consequences of this treatment of children. My challenge to that assumption has not been the standard one of claiming that children are far more capable than is commonly assumed and so we should treat children in the same way as adults. Rather, I have claimed that adults are far more vulnerable and lacking in capacity than we standardly give them credit and so we should treat adults in the same way as children. We all, adults and children, are equally vulnerable, lacking in capacity and in need of protection and support. What would that mean as practice? In this chapter I explore some of the consequences of this. It would require a fundamental reshaping of the law and so this chapter cannot provide a complete response to the question and only highlight some key features of a freshly rethought law. It would make a law which could treat adults and children in the same way to the benefit of both.

5.2 Our Image of the Legal Self

Legal rights and structures are shaped around a norm of what the self is like. The legal understanding of the person profoundly affects the kinds of legal rights we have. The law seems premised on a self which is independent, capacious and ration. Hence the law emphasises, as key rights, of autonomy, bodily integrity, privacy and liberty. Our right to be able to make our own choices over how to act; to only be subject to those responsibilities we choose to take, are seen as central pillars of the economic, social, and legal structures. The role for the law in such a model is to protect the individual from unwanted intrusions and to protect liberty to pursue one's goal for one's life. Anyone who falls outside the paradigm are described as 'vulnerable' and that terminology is used to monitor, supervise, and discipline them (Fineman 2012). They lack those essential skills to direct their own lives and protect themselves and so need others to do that for them.

If, however, we start with a norm of vulnerable, interdependent, caring people then the nature of legal intervention becomes different. The importance of upholding and maintaining those relationships becomes key. The law does not emphasize independence, liberty, and autonomy; but rather seeks to uphold relationships and care.

The significance of changing this image of the self is profound. To take one example: contract law. We are expected to be able be read contractual terms, understand them, and are taken to be bound by them. We are expected to be able to inspect and determine the quality of good before we buy them (the famous "caveat emptor" (let the buyer beware) rule). There are, in some cases, special provisions to deal with vulnerable contractors, but by and large contract law leaves people who are "foolish" enough to be taken in by rogues to fend for themselves. A contract law based around the norm of a vulnerable contractor might impose duties on us to look out for those we contract with, to enter into contracts in good faith, and not give effect to contracts where are clearly unfair to one side or the other (see Herring 2016a, b, Chap. 8).

This kind of approach can be taken more generally in the law. Dodds (2007, 501) argues:

> Attention to vulnerability ... changes citizens' ethical relations from those of independent actors carving out realms of rights against each other and the state, to those of mutually-dependent and vulnerability-exposed beings whose capacities to develop as subjects are directly and indirectly mediated by the conditions around them.

The acknowledgement of universal vulnerability also creates a different image of the legal relationship between the individual and the state. Rather than seeing the obligations of the state as owed towards a few particularly vulnerable citizens to meet their needs, it acknowledges that the institutions and provision of the state are used to meet the needs of all (Fineman 2010a, b). The question then becomes the extent to which the state meets all of our needs and which needs it chooses not to meet.

Fineman (2012) argues the role of institutions is important:

> This focus on institutions is to my mind one of the most significant aspects of the vulnerability analysis. Societal institutions are theorized as having grown up around

vulnerability. They are seen as interlocking and overlapping, creating layered possibilities of opportunities and support but also containing gaps and potential pitfalls. These institutions collectively form systems that play an important role in lessening, ameliorating, and compensating for vulnerability. Together and independently they provide us with resources in the form of advantages or coping mechanisms that cushion us when we are facing misfortune, disaster, and violence. Cumulatively, these assets provide individuals with resilience in the face of our shared vulnerability.

The argument here is that while a person or group may be identified as vulnerable as a result of a particular characteristic or body, it may in fact be the way institutional, economic, and social support is distributed that generates the vulnerability. In the face of universal vulnerability the needs of some are better met than the needs of others and so it may be if a particular group are disadvantaged that is not due to any vulnerability resting in them, but rather the allocation of social support. The response may not therefore be in seeking to address their 'weaknesses' but rather re-examining the distribution of support. Vast sums of money are spend on ensuring there are adequate sewerage and toileting provision for most people, but if an individual has particularly toileting needs, this can be seen as a special burden on the state, which might not be affordable.

5.3 Rights

The rights typically adopted by the law reflect the norm we have just described. The primary rights include those around autonomy, privacy and bodily integrity. They are designed to protect the individual from outside interference and pre-suppose and independent and autonomous self. It is not surprising that children are thought to be unsuitable recipients of such rights.

There are strong links between autonomy and vulnerability. Diduck (2013) argues that 'autonomy cannot exist without its "other", which in current rhetoric has become vulnerability. In the same way that autonomy may be the "friendly face" of individual responsibility, vulnerability may be the friendly face of dependence.' She argues that autonomy, the argument that people should be free to develop and live out their own version of the good life, is closely linked to the cliam that people are responsible for the choices that they make. Vulnerability is seen as the antithesis of this. Vulnerability is a state for which an individual is not to be blamed and is not accountable. Diduck (2013) argues that vulnerability 'implies disability, lack of capacity, of competence or victimhood, rather than the irresponsibility which tended to pervade dependency discourse'. The vulnerable person in this regard is to be treated as grateful for the protection and services of the state, which an autonomous person is normally spared.

Diduck (2013) in support of her claims about the use of vulnerability refers to a speech by David Cameron, which she suggest exemplifies the link between the concepts: 'We will look after the most vulnerable and needy. We will make the system simple. We'll make work pay. We'll help those who want to work, find work. But in return we expect people to take their responsibilities seriously too.' Diduck (2013) is however clear that she is suspicious of the elevation of autonomy that the vulnerability discourse permits. She argues autonomy is 'premised on the myth of a pre-existing equal playing field on which each individual has equal freedom, power and capacity to express it'. Her argument is that this claim is only plausible if an account can be provided for those who undoubtedly are unable to protect themselves. Vulnerability provides the language to account for the blatantly unautonomous, and leaves the norm of autonomy possible.

The current law fails to acknowledge, as argued in Chap. 4 that even if we have mental capacity our decision-making processes for all of us are flawed (Herring and Wall 2015). We take into account falsehoods; we are unduly influenced by others; we act in irrational ways. That is common and normal for everyone. The idea that we are governed by rational through plans we peruse to develop our vision of the good life seem palpably false, as I have argued elsewhere (Herring 2016a, b). That means that autonomy for everyone is hugely over-rated as a principle. We are all muddled, irrational, irascible, emotionally driven, incoherent thinkers and deciders. These are commonly associated with older people, but in fact it is true for us all (Herring 2016a, b). As the universal and beneficial model of vulnerability theory of vulnerability would claim, thank goodness we are not slaves of our mind or rational thought or logic. We are creatures of blood, love, wildness and eccentricity. We are not the product of rational thought nor do we want to be. The emphasis on autonomy unduly restricts us.

Returning to the issue of children, the emphasise the law generally places on autonomy means that generally people agree we need children's rights which will be separate from adult rights. Not everyone accepts that and the debate around children's rights is revealing. Children's liberationists (e.g. Holt 1974), who were particularly vocal in the 1970s, argued that children needed to be liberated from the tyranny of childhood. The argument went that children's ability to make decision for themselves was underestimated; deliberately so, it was claimed, because it meant that children could be kept as super-pets or super-slaves for the convenience of others. The child liberationist argument, then, went that children should have the same legal rights that adults had. For example, Holt (1974) argued for children having the right to vote, work, own property, receive minimum state education, use drugs and be able to consent to sexual relations.

Few commentators would now take such a position. If we were simply to give children the same rights as adults this would lead to the abuse and manipulation of children into activities that would be done for the benefit of others (Fortin 2009, 5). Just as the current system of rights leaves adults open to abuse and manipulation. It is commonly said, for example, that if children were given the same sexual rights as adults this would enable child abuse. This is true but ignores the manifold abuse of adults that our current regulation of sex permits.

Consider, for example, *A Local Authority v H* [2012] EWHC 49 (COP). The case concerned a young woman with learning difficulties known as H, who had come to the authority's attention when it was found tha queue of men and their animals were queuing up outside her flat for sex. Hedley J stated that "H's history demonstrates both a very early and a very deep degree of sexualisation" (para. 6). She had been on the child protection register and on the vulnerable adult register. At least one man had been convicted in respect of sexual offences against her. Hedley J

5.3 Rights

explained that 'others were engaging in sexual behaviour which, whilst consented to by her, could have been seen as unconventional and exploitative' (para 8). She had contracted a sexually transmitted disease (see para 28). Just before her admission to hospital the local authority reported:

> During this interview she gave an extensive, if confused, history of the willingness to have sex with anyone who asked her including strangers. She indicated that she was engaging in sex with multiple partners at the same time, including a group of much older men, considered that she was bi-sexual, and had engaged with oral and anal sex and that she had attempted to have sex with dog. (para 9)

Although eventually, and not without some difficulty given the state of the law, Hedley J was able to make an order seeking to protect her from exploitation. The protection came after a lengthy period of abuse. he law and practice had badly let down those suffering from mental disorders, allowing widespread sexual exploitation and abuse. Statistics on the extent of abuse are limited. In one leading study it was found that 61% of women with mental disorders were found to have suffered sexual abuse and 25% of men (McCarthy and Thompson 1996). A Mencap Report (2001) found that levels of sexual abuse among people with learning difficulties were four times higher than among the rest of the population (see Cambridge et al. (2011) for a helpful overview of current research). It seems that the current law and practice is failing to protect those with mental disability from abuse. A primary cause being that the law assume the people it is dealing with are autonomous, competent and able to look after themselves.

Returning to the debates over children's rights, a more moderate child liberationist claim, and one which would nowadays attract more support, would be that where children are as mature as an adult, we should treat the child in the same was as an adult. Further, that those areas where children are denied the rights that adults have, require a sufficient justification.

This leaves unanswered the question of how rights are to be understood. Some help can be found in the writing on children's rights. It is not possible to consider every model of children's rights. But I will focus on the work of one of the leading writers in this area: Eekelaar (1994), who is representative of many models. He argues that children have three types of interests: basic, developmental and autonomy interests. He explains that basic interests are children's claims concerning their physical, emotion and intellectual well-being. Developmental interests include children's claims to be able to maximise their potential, while an autonomy interest is 'the freedom to choose his own lifestyle and to enter social relations according to his own inclinations uncontrolled by the authority of the adult world, whether parents or institutions' (Eekelaar 1986, 170). He suggests that where there is a clash between these interests, basic and developmental should trump autonomy interests. There are two reasons for this ranking. First, he argues that we should consider how a child might retrospectively, as an adult, wish to be treated. He believes that most of us would not have wanted all our autonomy wishes to be granted as we were growing up, certainly not those that interfered with basic or developmental interests. Second, he argues that the ideal which we should be striving for is that the child develops into an 18 year-old with maximum autonomy. They will, then, have the maximum choice to decide for themselves how they wish to live their lives.

> [T]o bring a child to the threshold of adulthood with the maximum opportunities to form and pursue life goals which reflect as closely as possible an autonomous choice. (Eekelaar 1994)

Eekelaar argues that to achieve this, we need to ensure that during a childhood, the child's basic or developmental interests need to be protected, even where the child's autonomy interests point in a different direction. He argues, further, that enabling a child to have maximum autonomy in adulthood requires restrictions on their childhood now. It also requires that children be able to practice making decisions for themselves as they grow up. Children therefore must exercise autonomy in order to be able to have it later on. He also sees the exercise of autonomy by children as a marker of an open society:

> A society can be imagined whose members consider that autonomous self-determination by children, and indeed by the succeeding adult generation, is deemed to be in no one's interests. But such a society would not be an open society. It is a precondition for an open society that the exercise of autonomy by an agent is assumed to be in that agent's interests. And it is a precondition of believing that people have rights to hold that they have a right to achieve competence and articulate their self-interests (Eekelaar 1994, 87)

As Freeman (1992, 42) puts it:

> We would not be taking rights seriously if we only respected autonomy when we considered the agent was doing the right thing. But we also would be failing to recognise a child's integrity if we allowed him to choose an action, such as using heroin or choosing not to attend school, which could seriously and systematically impair the attainment of full personality and development subsequently.

And it is worth adding, of course, that not only are there extremely serious harms to adolescent sexual abuse, sexual penetrations carry risks even if consensual.

So, in summary the argument is this. If we accept a model of the kind promoted by John Eekelaar, there is an acceptance that some limitation can be imposed upon the autonomy of children, in the name of protecting their developmental or basic interests. These restrictions upon the autonomy of children are commonly justified in the name of promoting a child's autonomy later in life. My argument will be that, in broad terms, this kind of approach is a perfectly good version of rights for everyone. I have some difficulties with the details and style of presentation, but in the argument that follows I suggest it presents a way forward for basing adult's rights. If it is legitimate (and I accept it is) to restrict an eight year old's decisions on the basis it will impact on their eighteen year old self to an unacceptably harmful extent, cannot the same be said about the twenty one year old whose decision will impact on their thirty one year old self.

Eekelaar's model is that it is based around producing an autonomous eighteen year old. That is the overt justification for the model. However, this fails to recognise the value of child during adulthood. It seems premised on the model of childhood as a route to adulthood. It also appears to assume that once a person reaches 18 they cease to grow, develop and change. We can use his model as a model for life. At any point in life we are balancing the harm the decision will cause and the strength of the autonomous claim.

My primary concern with his model is that it seems to elevate interests in autonomy above all others. As argued in Chap. 5 we should be wary of seeing autonomy as the only important and significant value. We do not just want to be autonomous we want to be kind, generous, wonderful, having great relationships, achieve good things, and so forth. Autonomy has a role in these things, but it is premised on the individualised model of autonomy I am critiquing in this book.

My model of rights would therefore have the following features. First, we should recognise, as argued above, that our capacity to make decisions is flawed. There are particular concerns when a person is going to make a decision which will cause them harm or make a decision which will severely restrict how they wish to live. In such a case an awareness of the frailty of our capacity requires us to weigh up the harm caused by the decision and the extent to which can be regarded as autonomy. Coggon (2007, 236) helpful distinguishes three meanings of autonomy

1. Ideal desire autonomy—Leads to an action decided upon because it reflects what a person should want, measured by reference to some purportedly universal or objective standard of values.
2. Best desire autonomy—Leads to an action decided upon because it reflects a person's overall desire given his own values, even if this runs contrary to his immediate desire.
3. Current desire autonomy—Leads to an action decided upon because it reflects a person's immediate inclinations, ie what he thinks he wants in a given moment without further reflection.

As I am sure he would be the first to agree, even that is a simplification. It shows that autonomy is a not a binary concept. There can be some (I suggest very few) decisions which are richly autonomous: they are fully informed, and reflect a genuine part of the person's vision for their life and their settled values. Other decisions are only weakly informed, being made on a whim or with limited appreciation for the consequences of the decision.

I would add to this that in deciding whether a decision is worth of respect there is more to be asked than whether the decision is autonomous. We can also ask if respecting the decision will promote liberty, diversity, or dignity.

This enables an approach which involves weighing up the respect due to the decision, with the impact on the decision on the person. Where there is significant harm only a the most respect-worthy decisions respect can carry the day; where there is less harm involved, a less respect-worthy decision can be respected. This is an approach which can work for both adults and children.

However, I would want to add two further important aspects of that analysis, although readers would not need to make these additions in order to accept the general thrust of the argument.

First, I would argue in the weighing up whether a decision deserves respect, we must consider the importance of relationships. Relationships are, as argued throughout this book, central to our flourishing. But relationships, at least good relationships, involve give and take; responsibilities as well as rights. They do not let you take every decisions you wish. In seeking therefore the promotion of well-being and determining the extent to which the decision deserves respect we must look at the issue in its relational context (Herring 2013).

Second, as Charles Foster and I (2017) altruism and virtue are part of well-being, where they are shown to a reasonable extent. In considering the balance between respect due the decision and harm to the person the importance of showing a reasonable degree of virtue is an important part of that balance.

5.4 Divisions

One of the themes in this book is that universal vulnerability can challenge the divisions so emphasised by the law, between 'them and us'; the child and the adult; the competent and the not competent; the vulnerable and the non-vulnerable. These over-simplified categories lead to side-lining those who do not fall into them. As Bev Clough (2017) argues in relation to capacity:

> The creation of this stark binary perpetuates the 'othering' of those deemed to lack capacity, and justifies differential legal treatment. Those who do not fit neatly into this constructed binary fall outside of the margins.

It means that in seeking intervention or protection we need to recognize our own fallibility, weakness, and vulnerability to influence in determining what is the correct response. This is why the approach argued for in this book is not an argument for paternalism. It acknowledges that parents have much to learn from their children; doctors have much to discover from their patients; and that judges have much to learn from those who appear before them. A recognition of our mutual vulnerability requires us to come together to make decisions. To be making decisions together.

One of the dangers in seeking to separate the vulnerable and non-vulnerable is that it leads to an exaggeration. The distinction between adults and children is a find example of this.. There are a mass of social structures which push children towards a passive, non-autonomous role, and a mass of social structures which enable adults to live apparently independent and autonomous lives. These often go unnoticed and assumed as normal (Peterson and Wilkinson 2007). The division between the adults and children becomes reinforced and ignored. Each side fails to learn from and value the other.

5.5 Vulnerability and Care as Private

An important aspect of rethinking the relationship between children and adults is the role of care. Many writers on care have demonstrated that care of the 'vulnerable' is downgraded in modern legal and social thought (Herring 2013). It is seen as a private matter for individuals and their families to organized. Care is largely ignored or undervalued by the state and legal system. Part of that is because childhood is presented as time of care and adulthood an escape from that. One grows up to be self-sufficient and no longer in need of care.

That image is challenged by an acknowledgement that vulnerability is universal. To quote Fineman (2012) again:

> Privatization of dependency masks it, along with the other implications of human vulnerability and allows us to indulge in fantasies of independence, self-sufficiency, and autonomous agency. In an autonomous liberal subject analysis, if individuals or their private institutions fail, it is perceived as reflecting their weakness and incapacity, because the divide between public and private leaves them outside of general public or state responsibility—they occur in a separate sphere.

An acknowledgement of our universal vulnerability should go hand in hand with an acknowledgement of the importance of care work (Fineman 2004). Mutual care is essential for the functioning society. As Tronto (1993, 180) writes:

> Care is not a parochial concern of women, a type of secondary moral question, or the work of the least well off in society. Care is a central concern of human life. It is time we began to change our political and social institutions to reflect this truth.

Care work therefore needs to be recognised and valued within the legal system (Williams 2002).

The literature on ethics of care offers an ethical and legal approach which cementers the importance of care (Gilligan 1987; Friedman 1993; Sevenhuijsen 1998a, b; Groenhout 2004; Held 2006; Engster 2007; Herring 2013). There is an extensive literature on this and only a very brief summary will be offered here. These regard the role of law to promote caring relationships, rather than the pursuit of individual rights. Rights can be used in progressive ways of protecting and promoting values of community and mutuality. In failing to properly acknowledge care work, the law misses an important and inevitable aspect of life.

Ethics of care also shows the dangers of individualistic styles of reasoning. In relationships of caring and dependency our interests become intermingled (Shakespeare 2000, 2001). We do not break down into 'me' and 'you.' To harm a caregiver is to harm the person cared-for; to harm the person-cared for is to harm the caregiver. There should be no talk of balancing the interests of the caregiver and the person cared-for: the question rather should be emphasising the responsibilities they owe to each other in the context of a mutually supporting relationship Clement 1996, 11; Held 2006, Chap. 1).

Indeed, it is simplistic to imagine we can identify in a caring relationship who is the caregiver and who is the cared-for; their relationship is marked by interdependency. The 'cared-for' provides the 'caregiver' with gratitude, love, acknowledgement and emotional support, which will be of great emotional value to him. Indeed, often a 'caregiver' will be the 'cared-for' in another relationship. As Gibson (2005, 185) noted, our society is made up of overlapping networks of dependency. This is true of parents and children too.

This is why the welfare principle in the Children Act 1989, section 1, has to be treated with care. It appears to suggest that the interest of the child are paramount and that the interests of parents have no place in the courts reasoning. However, I have argued that it is impossible to isolate the interests of children from those of their parents in this way. The lives and intersts are entwined. I have recommended relationship-based welfare (Herring 2014, at 45–6), which

> must be understood to ask what order will be in [the child's] best interests understood within the context of the relationships they live in. That involves looking at what has happened in the relationships to date and what will happen in the future. It will acknowledge the care work that has been provided in the past and the value of that ... Under such an approach, cases can be resolved by recognising and acting in the child's interests whilst heeding carers' interests and the integrity of the family as a whole. If carers were to take every decision for the child considering only the child's welfare, that would not in fact promote the child's welfare. None of us would wish to be raised in a way that placed enormous burdens on our carers in order to promote our welfare, maybe just the tiniest bit. We would accept that decision might be made which on a particular occasion were not in our best interests, but which were part of a fair give and take in the relationships.

And this approach could be used in resolving any case where a determination as to a person's best interests is involved. That is because caring relations often involve a complex interplay of dependencies and vulnerabilities (Durham and Cannon 2008). As Fine and Glendinning (2005, 616) argued:

> Recent studies of care suggest that qualities of reciprocal dependence underlie much of what is termed 'care'. Rather than being a unidirectional activity in which an active care-giver does something to a passive and dependent recipient, these accounts suggest that care is best understood as the product or outcome of the relationship between two or more people.

When assessing the rights of any individual or the medical needs of an individual, such a person should be considered in a situational context. Never should it be a matter of assessing a person in isolation. Rather, each person's needs and rights must be considered in the context of their relationships.

5.6 Responsibilities to the Vulnerable

Politicians regularly talk about the vulnerable. It has become a cliché, although with considerable merit that 'the mark of any civilised society is how it protects the most vulnerable' (Smith 2009). Yet, this has proved a dangerous source of political intervention.

It has meant that in many political circles, vulnerable people need the help to escape from their vulnerability. This can quickly develop a coercive edge, so that a right to welfare support is conditional and seen as coming with responsibilities (Brown 2012). The goal and expectation is for everyone to be self-sufficient and independent (Wallbank and Herring 2014). We this too in the policies towards disabled people and carers often focussed on finding them routes into employment and self-sufficiency. These are not necessarily bad, but they are when they are presented as the total solution to the issues related to disability and care.

In some ways it used to reflect the difference between what used to be called the deserving and the undeserving poor. Brown (2012) suggests that the word 'vulnerable' can be a 'get out of jail free' card for those said to be responsible for their position or for getting themselves out of it. Vulnerability in this discourse becomes linked and associated with a lack of agency and responsibility.

Kate Brown draws out three themes from the political use of vulnerability:

(i) links between 'vulnerability', state power, and professional 'discretion';
(ii) the relationship of 'vulnerability' to citizenship; and
(iii) the vulnerable as 'deserving' of resources.

As to state power she sees vulnerability as a moral justification for 'social control mechanisms'. Professionals have the power to determine who is vulnerable and so what decisions should be made for them. Children, by being deemed vulnerable, require extra surveillance and restrictions. Some feminist writers claim that intervention in prostitution has been justified by deeming them to be vulnerable (Munro and Scoular 2012). Ironically, complying with an approved image of a vulnerable person can be a source of power. Brown (2012) claims that 'people who conform to commonly held notions of how 'vulnerable' people behave may find their entitlement to be more secure'. Hence, in terms of housing and mental health service provision the 'servile vulnerable person', who is grateful for help, will find themselves in a better position to access services. While those who resist the role and are 'difficult' will lose out on services.

An important aspect of focussing on universal vulnerability is that it highlights the importance of how social provision can ameliorate or magnify our vulnerability. We are all dependent on state welfare services or payments to meet our basic needs. The extent to which our needs are met by society will vary, enabling some to be much more resilient to their inherent vulnerability than others. This means we can re-examine how we understand disadvantaged groups. Rather than seeing them as people who have inherent weaknesses that cause them to be disabled, we can see that allocation of social resources have caused these disadvantages.

As Kitzinger (1997) suggests it means we can move from vulnerability to look at oppression. The danger is that use of power not only creates vulnerability it justifies it. To take one example, the corporal punishment of children is justified in the name of enabling parents to exercise control over children in order to protect them from risk. Yet the practice and acceptance of corporal punishment reveals a diminished acceptance of children's rights and personhood. It creates its own range of vulnerabilities. An appreciation of the common and interlocking vulnerabilities of adults and children can reveal what can otherwise be an unrecognized use of power.

The 'vulnerable' are seen as not fitting into the general discourse about personal responsibility and independence, which are promoted by the discourse of the new right, which sees the welfare state as a temporary safety net, primarily to be used to propel people back into work. In particular older people wish to avoid being seen as a burden on others or becoming dependent. In 2005 the Department of Health (2005) issued a new "vision" for older people entitled "Independence, Well-being and Choice". It clearly assuming that the ideal for old age would be a life marked by autonomy and independence. The message in Government publications and in the media is that by sensible life style choices; wishes financial investment and living properly then one can avoid the vulnerability and dependency that come with "bad ageing" (Boudiny 2013). Indeed if the dependency and vulnerability are a result of people's bad choices that can make the Government's responsibility less. Rather, as Lindsey (2016) puts it:

> the courts need to refocus and reformulate their definition of what being vulnerable means in the context of safeguarding and abuse, and shift their response away from the individual woman towards the harmful places and circumstances within which she is situated. I have argued that one way of achieving this is to target the perpetrators of abuse.

Under the universal and beneficial model of vulnerability, there is a recognition that we are all vulnerable. As Julie Wallbank and I (2014, 8) have argued:

> Vulnerabilities are not distributed equally among human beings. Although we share the commonality of being born, living lives and dying, the ways we live a vulnerable life are likely to be highly differentiated and affected by factors such as ethnicity, sexuality, gender, age, health, social class, employment status and care responsibilities. Indeed the range of factors impacting upon vulnerabilities is limitless.

An important part of focussing on vulnerability is that it highlights the importance of how social provision and ameliorate or magnify our vulnerability. That means our focus can shift from calling some people vulnerable to recognise that same people have more power. As Kitzinger (1997) suggests it means we can move from vulnerability to look at oppression. The danger is that use of power not only creates vulnerability it justifies it.

This can be particularly true in relation to children. To take one example, the corporal punishment of children justified in the name of enabling parents to exercise control over children in order to protect children from risk. Yet the practice and acceptance of corporal punishment reveals a diminished acceptance of children's rights and personhood. It creates its own range of vulnerabilities. An appreciation of the common and interlocking vulnerabilities of adults and children can reveal what can otherwise be an unrecognised use of power. The orthodox image of parent-child relationships also disguises the power that children can exercise over adults. An appreciation of the common and interlocking vulnerabilities of adults and children can reveal what can otherwise be an unrecognised use of power.

The acknowledgement of universal vulnerability also creates a different image of the legal relationship between the individual and the state. Rather than seeing the obligations of the state as owed towards a few particularly vulnerable citizen to meet their needs, it acknowledges that the institutions and provision of the state are used to meet the needs of all (Fineman 2010a, b). The question then becomes the extent to which the state meets all of our needs and which needs it chooses not to meet.

5.7 Age of Consent

It may be that even if you are convinced by the arguments up to here, that you believe that the law cannot take the kind of approach advocated. It is the curse, and the blessing, of the law that it has to draw lines. For example, he rule of law requires that the boundaries of what is or is not criminal are clearly defined, so that a person can predict with a degree of certainty whether their conduct will be criminal or not (Raz 1979). Clearly defined boundaries are also necessary to enable courts to deal with cases effectively. A good example is a speed limit. If the speed limit is set at 30 mph, then the driver knows precisely what speed they need to drive at to avoid a ticket. Similarly, if the driver exceeds that limit, the case can be easily dealt with at court. With modern technology, the speed of the driver is readily proved and a conviction or acquittal follows with the upmost efficiency. Contrast the alternative, an offence of 'travelling at a dangerous speed'. A driver would not know for sure if the speed they thought safe would be accepted as safe by a court. A police officer would have considerable discretion in deciding whom to arrest and court hearings would get bogged down with lengthy disputes over whether or not the speed was dangerous. Those kinds of arguments have persuaded legislatures in many countries to use "line drawing" offences in several ways.

Of course, such offences have a serious draw back. They can be seen as punishing harmless conduct in some cases. To return to the driving example, a person may be driving perfectly safely at 35 mph but still receive a ticket. Less often noticed, but also important, is that people may pose a harm but they may be on the "right side" of the line. A driver may be travelling at 26 mph, but that may be dangerously fast for those road conditions. In short, the clarity and efficiency of the bright line comes with 'errors' on either side of it.

It might, therefore, be argued that age can be properly be used as a bright line in law, even while it is acknowledged to be a fiction in reality. The age of consent to sex can be seen as a good example of age being used as a bright line criminal rule. Baroness Hale in *R v G* [2008] UKHL 37 (HL) [44] explained:

> Even if a child is fully capable of understanding and freely agreeing to such sexual activity, which may often be doubted, especially with a child under 13, the law says that it makes no difference. He or she is legally disabled from consenting.

As she emphasises, with such a legal presumption there is no claim that every child under a particular age *in fact* has capacity to consent (although she may well), but rather that there are sound policy reasons justifying the presumption. In other words that despite all the arguments used so far, when it comes to hard law, whether we like it or not age returns as a practical necessity.

Bright legal line drawing based on age is common in the law generally. Age is regularly used by the law to mark out when a person may or may not be permitted to engage in activities ranging from buying alcohol to getting married (Herring 2003). While not always explicitly stated, this is normally done on the basis that the child is legally presumed to lack the capacity to make the decision. There may be other factors at play too, such as alcohol having a greater impact on a younger body than an older one. Whenever they are used, it must be accepted (as it usually is in cases of legal line drawing) that there will be cases where people below the particular age are deemed to lack the capacity to consent, even though in fact they do have that capacity. Why are such presumptions used, if we know that there are cases where they will be incorrect?

I suggest that line drawing of this kind with regard to age requires us to consider the following:

1. Is this a situation which is better resolved by individual assessment in the particular circumstance, rather than drawing a line?
2. At what age should the line be drawn?

The first question will be answered yes in many medical cases. A child who is seeking medical treatment can readily be assessed by their doctor at the same time. Given the gravity of the issue there is no reason why age should be used as a proxy. But might there be other areas where this approach is not possible. The most obvious contender would be sexual offences.

There are three key differences between a doctor treating a minor patient and a person wanting to have sex with a minor. The first is that a medical professional has the expertise to make the kind of nuanced assessment of the capacity of the person that we would want. Indeed, if the question of a minor's capacity to understand an issue were to go to court, the evidence of a medical professional would be key. By contrast, an ordinary person who wants to have sex with a minor has no skills or expertise to make an assessment of their minor partner's capacity.

The second is that while the medical professional, we might take it, has no personal stake in whether their patient does or does not have capacity, they will want what is best for their patient and will make their assessment in the best way they can, while having nothing to gain from the outcome. By contrast, the person who wants to have sex with an underage partner is obviously biased in their assessment of capacity.

The third is that the doctor has the time, clarity of thought and space to make the necessary assessment. The person at the start of a sexual encounter is unlikely to have the kind of cool detachment to make a full assessment of capacity. A doctor will have a set of professional guidelines to follow in order to ensure she has made an appropriate assessment. The person wishing to have sex with an underage child has little to go on to perform his assessment.

5.7 Age of Consent

With these points in mind, it becomes clear that saying to a person who wants to have sex with a minor, 'well you should make an assessment of their capacity', is unlikely to result in an accurate assessment or to provide sufficiently clear guidance to the would-be participant in sexual penetration. Duff (2002), arguing in favour of such bright lines, provides a detailed analysis in support of them. He explains that there are certain dangerous activities where people cannot be trusted and should not trust themselves to decide whether the activity is safe. He (Duff 2002, 103) writes:

> A man excited at the prospect of sex with a young woman is ill placed to judge her maturity; a driver in a hurry is ill placed to judge how fast it is safe for her to drive; and someone relaxing in a pub is ill placed to judge whether another drink might impair his capacity to drive safely. We recognise the need for some kind of regulation in these spheres, because we cannot trust each other, or ourselves, to decide in these contexts whether we can safely engage in a proposed action (having sexual intercourse with this young person; driving at this speed, or after having this many drinks).

He goes on to say that there will be defendants who insist that their partner is below the age of consent but that they have the maturity to make the decision nevertheless. Yet he says of such a defendant, 'he does not know that he knows this' and if he goes ahead based on his own judgement, he takes an unjustified risk that he is wrong and

> arrogantly claims the right to decide for himself on matters which he, like the rest of us, should not trust himself to decide. His claim is arrogant because it is unjustified — but also because it seeks to set him above his fellow citizens, in matters which affect their legally protected interests; and that is what merits the censure of the criminal law. (Duff 2002, 103)

This seems compelling. Yet, they seem just as compelling when the interaction is with an adult. The solution of using a sharp age divide for children to protect them from exploitation, but leaving adults to be assessed by each other in an equally flawed way seems undesirable. I would suggest the reason why we need an age of consent is the inadequacy of the law on consent to sexual offences in relation to adults. This is not the place to explore all of the failures of the current law to do this (Herring 2017). But I would argue that a law which started with a recognition that we are vulnerable and have responsibilities to respect each other's sexual autonomy could much more adequately protect everyone's autonomy than one based on assumptions based on age.

5.8 Conclusion

This chapter has considered the claims made about the vulnerability of children and explored the impact that the perceived vulnerability of children has had on the legal responses to children. While sympathetic to the writings which have sought to deny the vulnerability of children, this chapter has sought rather to empahsise the vulnerability of adults. It has argued that vulnerability is the common lot of humanity. The portrayal by adults of children as especially vulnerable is part an attempt to hide from the vulnerability of adults. It helps bolster the image of the autonomous independent man on which so much legal analysis and thought is based. He is the figure who so dominates the law books and law courses. The more realistic picture of the vulnerable interdependent relationship is sidelined and overlooked. Yet that is our reality. We need to rejoice in our vulnerability, for it is that which is central to our humanity. Our law needs to centralize common human vulnerability and the resulting need for networks of care, as the cornerstone of a legal system.

References

Boudiny K (2013) 'Active Ageing': from empty rhetoric to effective policy tool. Ageing Soc 33 (6):1077–1098
Brown K (2012) Re-moralising "Vulnerability". People Place Policy Online 6:41–65
Cambridge P et al (2011) Patterns of risk in adult protection referrals for sexual abuse and people with intellectual disability. J Appl Res Intellect Disabil 24(2):118–132
Clement G (1996) Care, autonomy and justice: feminism and the ethic of care. Westview Press, Boulder, Colerado
Clough B (2017) Disability and vulnerability: challenging the capacity/incapacity binary. Soc Policy Soc 16:469–481
Coggon J (2007) Varied and principled understandings of autonomy in english law: justifiable inconsistency or blinkered moralism? Health Care Anal 15:235–257
Department of Health (2005) Independence, well-being and choice. Our vision for the future of social care in England Department of Health, London
Diduck A (2013) Autonomy and vulnerability in family law: the missing link. In: Wallbank J, Herring J (eds) Vulnerabilities, care and family law. Routledge, Abingdon
Dodds S (2007) Depending on care: recognition of vulnerability and the social contribution of care provision. Bioethics 21:500–535
Duff A (2002) Crime, prohibition, and punishment. J Appl Philos 19:97–119
Dunham CC, Cannon JH (2008) 'They're still in control enough to be in control': paradox of power in dementia caregiving. J Aging Stud 22:45–65
Eekelaar J (1986) The emergence of children's rights. Oxf J Legal Stud 6:161–186
Eekelaar J (1994) The interests of the child and the child's wishes: the role of dynamic self-determinism. Int J Law Policy Fam 8:42–68
Engster D (2007) The heart of justice. Care ethics and political theory. Oxford University Press, Oxfod
Fine M, Glendinning C (2005) Dependence, independence or interdependence? Revisiting the concepts of 'care' and 'dependency. Ageing Soc 21:601–631
Fineman M (2004) The autonomy myth. New Press, New York
Fineman M (2008) The vulnerable subject: anchoring equality in the human condition. Yale Law Feminism 20:1–81
Fineman M (2010a) The vulnerable subject and the responsive state. Emory Law J 60:251–298
Fineman M (2010) Equality: still illusive after all these years. In: Grossman J, McClain L (eds) Social citizenship and gender. Cambridge
Fineman M (2012) "Elderly" as vulnerable: rethinking the nature of individual and societal responsibility. Elder Law Rev 17:23–65
Fortin J (2009) Children's rights and the developing law. Cambridge University Press, Cambridge
Foster C, Herring J (2017) Atruism, welfare and the law. Springer, London
Freeman M (1992) Taking children's rights more seriously. Int J Law Policy Fam 12:42–71

References

Friedman M (1993) Liberating care. In: Friedman M (ed) What are friends for?. Cornell University Press, Ithica, New York

Gibson D (2005) Aged care: old policies, new solutions. Cambridge University Press, Cambridge

Gilligan C (1987) Moral orientation and moral development. In: Kittay E, Meyers D (eds) Women and moral theory. Rowman and Littlefield, Savage, Maryland

Groenhout R (2004) Connected lives: human nature and an ethics of care. Rowman and Littlefield, Savage, Maryland

Held V (2006) The ethics of care. Oxford University Press, New York

Herring J (2003) Children's rights for grown ups. In: Fredman S, Spencer S (eds) Age as an equality issue. Hart, Oxford

Herring J (2008) Caregivers in medical law and ethics. J Contemp Health Law Policy 25:1–31

Herring J (2013) Caring and the law. Hart, Oxford

Herring J (2014) Relational autonomy and family law. Springer, London

Herring J (2016a) Vulnerable adults and the law. Oxford University Press, Oxford

Herring, J (2016) Peter Skegg and the question no-one asks: why presume capacity? In: Wall J, Henaghan M (eds) Law, ethics and medicine. Thomson, Auckland

Herring J (2017) Relational autonomy and consent. In: Reed A, Bohlander M, Wake N, Smith E (eds) Consent. Routledge, UK

Herring J, Wall J (2015) Autonomy, capacity and vulnerable adults: filling the gaps in the Mental Capacity Act. Legal Stud, 698–719

Holt J (1974) Escape from childhood. Pelican, London

Kittay EF (2005) Equality, dignity and disability. In: Lyons M, Waldron F (eds) Perspectives on equality. Liffey Press, Dublin

Kittay F (2011) The ethics of care, dependence, and disability. 44 Ratio Juris 49

Kitzinger S (1997) 'Who are you kidding? Children, power and the struggle against sexual abuse. In: James A, Prout A (eds) Constructing and reconstructing childhood. Routledge, Abingdon

Lindsey J (2016) Developing vulnerability: a situational response to the abuse of women with mental disabilities. Feminist Legal Stud 24:295–314

McCarthy M, Thompson D (1996) Sexual abuse by design: an examination of the issues in learning disability services. Disabil Soc 11(2):205

Mencap (2001) Behind closed doors. Mencap, London

Munro V, Scoular J (2012) Abusing vulnerability? Contemporary law and policy responses to sex work and sex trafficking in the UK. Feminist Legal Stud 20(3):189–206

Peterson A, Wilkinson I (2007) Health, risk and vulnerability. Routledge, Abingdon

Raz J (1979) The authority of law. Oxford University Press, Oxford

Sevenhuijsen S (1998) Too good to be true? (IWM Working Paper No. 3/1998)

Sevenhuijsen S (1998b) Citizenship and the ethics of care. Routledge, London

Shakespeare (2000) Help. Verso, London

Shakespeare T (2001) The social relations of care. In: Lewis G, Gewirtz S, Clarke J (eds) Rethinking social policy. Policy Press, Bristol

Smith J (2009) Speech: Hansard HC vol 486 col 524 (19 January 2009)

Tronto J (1993) Moral boundaries: a political argument for an ethic of care. Psychology Press, London

Wallbank J, Herring J (2013) Introduction. In: Wallbank J, Herring J (eds) Vulnerability care and family law. Routledge, Abingdon

Williams F (2002) The presence of feminism in the future of welfare. Econ Soc 31:502–524

Mackenzie C, Rogers W, Dodds S (eds) (2014) Vulnerability: new essays in ethics and feminist philosophy. Oxford University Press, Oxford

Chapter 6
Vulnerability Is Good

Abstract This final chapter will argue that the common perception that vulnerability is an undesirable and stigmatic characteristic is misguided. Rather we should rejoice in our universal vulnerability. It requires us to reach out to others and work together to find mutual solutions to our common challenges. Our vulnerability means we must be open to change and rethinking who we are. It means we find our identity and meaning through and with others, rather than in our own abilities.

Keywords Vulnerability · Relationships · Personhood · Co-operation
Virtue · Goods

6.1 The Good of Vulnerability

Vulnerability is often seen in public discourse as an undesirable state to be in. It implies weakness and an inability to look after yourself. People should avoid becoming vulnerable and if you are vulnerable the state should enable you to escape from your vulnerability. This chapter will claim the opposite. We should rejoice in our vulnerability. It our pretence that it is only children who are vulnerable and we adults who need to grow out of vulnerability, that is a tragedy. This will be explored in this chapter.

The common negative attitude to towards vulnerability and dependency is well captured by John Moore, who as the Secretary of State for Social Security State (quoted Fine and Glendinning 2005), commented:

> A climate of dependence can in time corrupt the human spirit. Everyone knows the sullen apathy of dependence and can compare it with the sheer delight of personal achievement.

As Shildrick (2002, 71) noted that, 'in western modernity at least, vulnerability is figured as a shortcoming, an impending failure'.

England now has a Secretary of State for Vulnerability. Revealingly Sarah Newton's full title is Parliamentary Under Secretary of State for Vulnerability, Safeguarding and Countering Extremism. The grouping of these three topics in her title is revealing. It reinforces the view that vulnerability impacts on on particular deficient groups. Indeed, my search of gov.co.uk found 7038 hits of government programmes particularly aimed at groups of vulnerable people covering everything from oral health needs to the dangers of Nitrates.

Vulnerability in childhood is seen as something that children should grow up and escape from. As Archard (2001, 52) has written:

> 'There may be features of childhood but not of adulthood which are valuable, such as innocence, wonder and trust. There may, correspondingly be features of adulthood but not childhood which are valuable, such as experience and independence. It is also evident that there may be features of childhood but not of adulthood which are not valuable, such as dependence and vulnerability'.

This is, I suggest, profoundly mistaken. Given vulnearability and dependence are inevitable goods they should be accepted and acknowledged. More than that, they are greatly to be welcomed. They are often virtues, not vices. This chapter will focus on establishing that claim.

I have argued earlier in Chap. 4 that vulnerability and interdependence is an inevitable feature of being human (Dodds 2005). Something has gone very wrong with our care of vulnerable older people when 'not being a burden' is reported as the main goal of their lives by patients living in nursing homes (Pleschberge 2007). Dependency and co-operation are innately human activities. From our earliest beginnings we are in relationships of dependency and we continue so for much, if not all, of our lives. Sometimes receiving, sometimes giving, care; often doing both. Relationships of dependency are central to our lives.

Being vulnerable is an aspect of many of the great values. Those things which make us vulnerability: our interdependence, our relationality; our need for care, are all great values (Harris 1997). Let me develop those a little more.

6.2 Vulnerability and Co-operation

Our mutual vulnerability requires us to reach out to others to offer and receive help from them. The virtues of beneficence and compassion are encouraged and necessary. We have to become open to others and our own and other's needs. A recognition of our mutual vulnerability leads to empathy and understanding (Kittay 2011). It creates intimacy and trust. It compels us to focus on interactive, co-operative solutions to the issues we address. It encourages creativity in finding new ways of overcoming our human limitations and requires a desire to accept others as they are. As Carse (2006, 48) puts it: 'Our vulnerability is inextricably tied to our capacity to give of ourselves to others, to treasure and aspire, to commit to endeavors, to care about justice and about our own and other's dignity.'

The great achievements of the human race are rarely, if ever, the result of the efforts of a single person. They result from co-operation and mutual endeavour. Whether it is in terms of education; construction; transport, or health care it is people combining their skills that produce the most effective responses.

The current political use of vulnerability narrative tends to promote disablist approaches to the issue (Fine and Glendinning 2005). As many writers of disabilities studies have written, there is great pressure to be perceived as independent and lacking vulnerability. Success for a person with a disability is measured by the extent to which they may be able to be (or present themselves as being) independent and autonomous. In short, to be 'normal' (Shakespeare 2000). But that is a completely wrong misuse of the concept. The vulnerability approach promoted in this chapter recognizes the disability in all of us. It recognizes that all of us need social provision; we all need help. It can only be in our joining together and co-operation that human flourishing can be found. We may have different needs and different strengths. Our vulnerabilities are manifest in different ways. So, our mutual vulnerability encourages us to come together and recognise and value the different gifts, and limitation, that we all have.

6.3 Vulnerability and Change

Recognising our vulnerability and the vulnerability to others requires use to be open to the world. Our vulnerable selves are dependent, as I have already said, on our mutable bodies and our changing relationships, and inevitability this means they are dynamic and must be open to unpredictable change. As Nussbaum (2001) has argued, such relational goods require 'openness towards the world and its possibilities … a yielding and receptive character of soul that is not compatible with an undue emphasis on self-protection.' And that is good. It means our lives have a journey and alter as our relationships, responsibilities and bodies change. It stops us getting "into a rut". As Gilson (2013) argues, is an 'open-ended condition that makes possible learning, love, affection, and self-transformation just as much as it makes possible suffering and harm'. It is true that with this unknown openness to the unbidden can come good and bad things.

6.4 Vulnerability and Relationships

Relationships are central to human thriving. A life without relationships and without friendship would not be a good life. Yet relationships rely on us being willing to be vulnerable and thrive from our vulnerability. Relationships involve undertaking trust, assuming responsibility fo others; and having an obligations to care. These all create vulnerability:

> we are in danger of not meeting our obligations; we are risk of others not meeting theirs to us. Relationship can be used as a tool of abuse and in relationships we are open to being abused (Sevenhuijsen 1998).

Relationships; intimacy; care; all of these things in their nature render us vulnerable (Harris 1997). Exclusion of the other to achieve invulnerability is an anathema to relationships. Our vulnerability, further, requires us to meet out to others to meet their needs and to have our needs met. Our very vulnerability provides us with the seeds for our growth through relationships with others (Fineman 2012).

Vulnerability is essential to relationships. In entering a relationship with others this creates an understanding of trust, the assumptions of responsibility, and obligations of care. These things create a vulnerability: we are in danger of not meeting our obligations; we are risk of others not meeting theirs to us. Our trust might be misplaced. The opening up of our natures creates a risk we will be taken advantage of, that private information will be used to harm us, and the risk of grief and loss (Sevenhuijsen 1998). Yet relationships are good and beneficial. Indeed they may well be described as one of the basic goods. Relationships, intimacy, care; all of these things in their nature render us vulnerable (Harris 1997). Exclusion of the other to achieve invulnerability is an anathema to relationships. As Phillips (2011, 139) puts it:

> Helplessness is the precondition for human bonds, for exchange; you have to be a helpless subject in order to be helped, in order to be understood, in order to become a moral creature. And so, by the same token, if you can't experience helplessness you are precluded from these fundamental human experiences.

For those who see the self in a relational way then the separation of the 'Other', with the rejection of vulnerability that goes with that leads to a denial of the self. As Butler (2004, 22) puts it:

> It is not as if an 'I' exists independently over here and then simply loses a 'you' over there, especially if the attachment to 'you' is part of what composes who 'I' am. If I lose you, under these conditions, then I not only mourn the loss, but I become inscrutable to myself. Who 'am' I, without you? When we lose some of these ties by which we are constituted, we do not know who we are or what to do. On one level, I think that I have lost 'you' only to discover that 'I' have gone missing as well. At another level, perhaps what I have lost 'in' you, that for which I have no ready vocabulary, is a relationality that is composed neither exclusively of myself nor you, but is to be conceived as the tie by which those terms are differentiated and related.

Imagine the live of a Stoic, who renders himself invulnerable to the blow of fortune and safe from the 'slings and arrows' of life. That would not be a life we expect to be marked by virtue, it would lack empathy (Card 1998). The ability to provide deep care for others and a lack of investment in the well-being of others. No love. If relations with others is what produces identity then identity is inherently vulnerable, but not in a bad way (Drichel 2013). To quote Butler again:

> One does not always stay intact. One may want to, or manage to for a while, but despite one's best efforts, one is undone, in the face of the other, by the touch, by the scent, by the feel, by the prospect of the touch, by the memory of the feel (Butler 2004).

Our vulnerability, further, requires us to reach out to others to meet their needs and to have our needs met. These interactions are fulfilling and creative. Our very vulnerability provides us with the seeds for our growth through relationships with others (Fineman 2010).

6.5 Vulnerability and Personhood

There is much debate around the concept of personhood in ethics. This, somewhat misleading term, is designed to capture what generates the highest moral claim. The idea is that persons are entitled to the strongest legal protections (human rights) and the highest moral standing. Those deemed non-person may have some protected interests, but at a lesser level than persons.

The debate is interesting because it raises a key question about what it is we particularly value about humanity. It is not possible to discuss this debate fully here, I have discussed it at length elsewhere (Foster and Herring 2017). To some commentators it is our rationality and our intellectual capabilities which generate personhood. However, doing so excludes those with severe cognitive impairments from the status. The argument I have developed with Charles Foster is that our source of value, dignity and humanity is not our intellect but our feelings, relationships, care, love. It is because we are vulnerable that we come to value not our separate personal capacities but the relations between us. And love is therefore at the heart of human thriving. As Mary Neale argues:

> We are beings who strive for—and achieve—the sublime, the awe-inspiring, and the transcendent. We aspire to be, not just animals, but moral beings: to pursue second order preferences and desires; to hold ourselves and others to standards of behaviour that surpass those we tolerate from other animals and would settle for from ourselves if we were content to fulfil only the animal side of our nature; and we characteristically hope for immortality, either in the literal sense of "life after death", or in a secular sense through the legacies of our work (art, invention, discovery) and the personal marks we leave on those whose lives have intersected with our own (we wish not to be forgotten).

The argument that it is our relationships that generate the highest moral status, rather than our intellect our autonomy, is important. It shows that young and old, able-minded and those of limited intellectual ability, the disabled and the abled-bodied are all equally valuable because our vulnerabilities require us to be in relationships.

6.6 Conclusion

Our society is in danger of devaluing those who are seen to be vulnerable. The stereotype of old age: mental and physical frailty; dependence on others; gullibility; terror of loneliness are the reality we all face and cope with throughout our lives. The stereotype of childhood: innocent, weak, ignorant and pliable are also the reality we all face and cope with throughout our lives. The universal and beneficial model of vulnerability suggests that we are all, regardless of age presenting an image of good physical and mental health; emotional security; sound judgement; controlled bodies. It is, ironically, only in old age that the stereotypes match the reality. Yet by then we have been hiding and denying that reality for too long.

In this chapter, and throughout this book acknowledging these realities about our vulnerabilities will give us a truer sense of our selves; a more effective legal response; and open up the goods of co-operation, change and relationships. We need to throw off the shackles of adulthood, acknowledge the childishness of us all, and rejoice in the vulnerability of every human person.

References

Archard D (2001) Philosophical perspectives on childhood. In: Fiona J (ed) Legal concepts of childhood. Oxford University Press, Oxford
Butler J (2004) Precarious life. Verso, London
Card C (1998) Stoicism, evil and the possibility of morality. Metaphilosophy 29:245–271
Carse A (2006) Vulnerability, agency and human flourishing. In: Dell'Oro R (ed) Taylor C. Health and Human Flourishing Georgetown University Press, Washington
Drichel S (2013) Reframing vulnerability: "So Obviously the Problem…?"Subst 42:3–25
Dodds S (2005) Gender, ageing, and injustice: social and political contexts of bioethics. J Med Ethics 31:295–304
Fine M, Glendinning C (2005) Dependence, independence or interdependence? Revisiting the concepts of 'care' and 'dependency. Ageing Soc 21:601–631
Fineman N (2010) The vulnerable subject and the responsive state. Emory Law J 60:251–298
Fineman M (2012) "Elderly" as vulnerable: rethinking the nature of indivdviual and societal responsibility. Elder Law Rev 17:23–65
Foster C, Herring J (2017) Identity. Personhood and the Law, Springer, London
Gilson E (2013) The ethics of vulnerability: a feminist analysis of social life and practice. Routledge, New York
Harris G (1997) Dignity and vulnerability. California, Berkeley
Kittay EF (2011) The ethics of care, dependence, and disability. Ratio Juris 44–49
Nussbaum M (2001) The fragility of goodness: luck and ethics in Greek tragedy and philosophy. Cambridge University Press, Cambridge
Phillips A (2011) Freud's helplessness. In: Levine G (ed) The joy of secularism. Princeton University Press, Princeton NJ
Pleschberge S (2007) Dignity and the challenge of dying in nursing homes: the residents' view. Age Ageing 36:197–215
Sevenhuijsen S (1998) Citizenship and the ethics of care. Routledge, London
Shakespeare T (2000) Help. Verso, London
Shildrick M (2002) Embodying the monster: encounters with the vulnerable self. Routledge, London

Printed by Printforce, United Kingdom